THE 3 PERSONAL B
THAT NEARLY

PROMOTE YOUR D@MN SELF.™

LinkedIn Users, Pay Close Attention to #2

 Shantel Love

MBA

Reviews of Promote Your D@mn Self: The 3 Personal Branding Mistakes to Avoid That Nearly Destroyed My Career

"After being part of the 'Promote Your Damn Self' community and receiving coaching from Shantel, I knew I had to read her book. As an introverted marketer, I had always been content with going along to get along in my career. That all changed when I was laid off. Taking Shantel's advice, I finally 'Promoted My Damn Self.' The results were remarkable: I landed a new role with a +35% pay increase and secured $500K in sponsorship for my new project. Shantel is not only incredibly knowledgeable but also easy to talk to. Her guidance was invaluable in transforming my career."

Monica G- *Events Coordinator*- Education Technology Industry

"There are so many posts and advice I see everyday about how to leverage LinkedIn and I was pleasantly surprised by how easy to read and action oriented this book is. The information went beyond the typical advice and really leaned into ways to develop yourself as a thought leader and tap into the power of your voice. The templates are very helpful. It was a reminder that I already have one of the most powerful tools to build my future with."

Corean C- *Co-Founder, Chief Experience Officer*- Shift to Play

"After years of watching peers get promotion after promotion, albeit well deserved, I decided it was time to stop watching and congratulating and start taking ownership of my own trajectory. It's ludicrous that I have been a marketer for half a decade, but I have never considered myself a brand. Shantel's Promote Your Damn Self has been my proverbial bible during this transformation. Using Shantel's actional advice, I have the confidence and strategies to be the corporate "It Girl", I have always admired and within one quarter of applying the tools in this book, my manager has noticed my newfound confidence and gravitas and I am well on my way to a promotion this fiscal year. On top of that, I have been able to leverage my LinkedIn presence to curate a brand within my company and externally. So do it! Get the book, and Promote Your Damn Self."

Whitney Y- *Senior Product Marketing*- LinkedIn

"I can imagine that (Promote Your Damn Self) is the thing she says to herself every morning since the day she started to own and cultivate her personal brand. Through it, she's found her mission to help others find theirs. Shantel provides practical and attainable strategies for leveraging LinkedIn to develop your voice while also articulating the concerns and fears around stepping out and doing the damn thing."

Keishla C-J- *Customer Success Leader*-

Reviews of Promote Your D@mn Self: The 3 Personal Branding Mistakes to Avoid That Nearly Destroyed My Career

"Shantel was able to give us the perfect framework to get started with monetizing our voice not only on LinkedIn but in every aspect of our career. Her framework includes real stories and templates to follow as well as ways to get started today!"

Nichole T- *Enterprise Customer Success Manager-*Tech Industry

"I wish I had Shantel's expertise when I first joined LinkedIn; it would have saved me wasted time and effort. Shantel is an expert, honest friend, and professional cheerleader all rolled into one. She tells you what you want to know, in the way you want to hear it, while encouraging you to take action. This is a must-have guide for both career professionals and entrepreneurs."

Elizabeth S- *Executive Director* - Human Tech Institute

"...love the intention of speaking to those negative feelings and how to counter them with the small wins or even borrowing them as I did from your coaching for my first speaking engagement. I am beyond a fan of the exercises given and how you personally walked through what we now know as 'Promote Your D@mn Self' starter to advanced kit. "

Terrence C- *Operations Manager-* Pearson

"Your insights made me realize that merging my natural gift of supporting women and girls through coaching, mentoring, and teaching with my career—focused on systems change and identifying what works within those systems—was something I hadn't fully embraced. Our conversations helped me see that I was hiding, and your chapter illuminated the mental models I held that kept me from recognizing this. I was stuck in rationalization."

Tiffany W- *Director-* The Miami Foundation

Shantel Love is the expert at helping people find their voice, hone their stories, gain confidence and courage, and start. This book will give you the confidence and clarity you need to do so not just for yourself, but for everyone who will benefit from reading the content that YOU have created.

Jen L- *CEO-* Success Mindset Mentor

I anticipated some motivating words from an experienced leader on monetizing one's skillset. Shantel not only offers encouragement and compelling stories but also provides practical templates and examples to help you get started. This book is truly a game changer.

Shameka S- *Senior CSM-* Powerschool

PROMOTE YOUR D@MN SELF™

PROMOTE YOUR D@MN SELF™

The 3 Personal Branding Mistakes to Avoid That Nearly Destroyed My Career.
LinkedIn™ Users, Pay Close Attention to #2

Shantel Love, MBA

COPYRIGHT NOTICE

Copyright © 2024 Shantel Love LLC.

All rights reserved. No part of this publication may be reproduced, distributed, or transmitted in any form or by any means, including photocopying, recording, or other electronic or mechanical methods, without the prior written permission of the publisher, except in the case of brief quotations embodied in critical reviews and certain other noncommercial uses permitted by copyright law. For permission requests, write to the publisher, addressed "Attention: Permissions Coordinator," at the address below.

ISBN: 979-8-218-49801-6 (Paperback)

Front cover image by Shantel Love.
Book design by Shantel Love.

First printing edition 2024.

Shantel Love LLC Publisher
Henderson, NV, 89011

www.shantellove.com

DEDICATION

To my loving and supportive husband, Quintin Love, Ph.D., and my little firecracker of a son, Isaiah Love: This one's for you. You've been my backbone, my cheerleaders, and my reality check all rolled into one. You believed in me as I stepped into the role of becoming the mentor I never had. Your love has shaped me into the powerhouse that I am today. I owe you both more than words can say.

Table of CONTENTS

Prologue: Why I Wrote This Book..I

Chapter 1

Promote Your D@mn Self: Because No One Else Will Do It For You...............1

Yesterday's LinkedIn is Not Today's LinkedIn..................................10

Chapter 2

Amplify Your Inner Confidence: Building a Confident Personal Brand........27

Avoid Personal Branding Mistake #1..38

Chapter 3

Navigate LinkedIn Confidently: Thriving Under Your Boss's Watchful Eye...51

Chapter 4

Sculpt Your Unique Brand Identity: Mastering..........................81
the "Me, Myself, and I"

Start with taking this Personal Branding Assessment........................87

The Challenges of Personal Branding- Imposter Syndrome.................92

The Challenges of Personal Branding- Systemic Challenges...................95

xiii

Table of CONTENTS

Chapter 5

Write Your Success Story: Becoming a Thought Leader on LinkedIn.......103

Avoid Personal Branding Mistake #2..104

7 steps to Promote Your D@mn Self as a Thought Leader on LinkedIn...108

Thought Leadership Checklist........ 126

Chapter 6

Empower Your Skillset: Monetizing Your Expertise 133

in your career and on LinkedIn

Avoid Personal Branding Mistake #3..134

Monetizing Your Career..150

Chapter 7

Reel Them In: Mastering Attention-Grabbing LinkedIn Content..........175

Chapter 8

Personal Brand Building as a Job Seeker...193

Chapter 9

The A.N.S.W.E.R. is within YOU..213

SELF-PROMOTION ISN'T BRAGGING; IT'S INVITING OTHERS TO BENEFIT FROM YOUR UNIQUE GIFTS.

WHY I WROTE THIS?

You know how sometimes you stumble upon something amazing and think, "Dang, why didn't anyone tell me about this sooner?" That's exactly how I felt about personal branding and LinkedIn, and I bet you might feel the same way.

What's this book all about? It's the no-gatekeeping guide to building your personal brand, growing your career, and leveraging LinkedIn that I wish someone had slapped into my hands years ago. If you're sitting there thinking LinkedIn is just another social media time-suck, think again friend, because I'm about to blow your mind.

This book? I've taken my blood, sweat, and tears (okay, maybe not blood, but definitely some late-nights) and poured them into these pages. I will expose the 3 Personal Branding Mistakes to Avoid That Nearly Destroyed My Career. I'm talking real stories, real experiences, and real "wowwww, I wish I'd known that" moments. Don't worry, I've changed the names to protect the innocent (and the not-so-innocent).

I wrote Promote Your D@mn Self because I care too much NOT to empower you. I could have called this book "encourage yourself" but I need you to understand the call to action here. This isn't just another "how-to" book. It's a complete system for personal branding, career, and LinkedIn success, created by a successful corporate executive and entrepreneur who's been in your shoes and knows exactly how to overcome the unique challenges you're facing.

I'm about to let you in on secrets that will change your entire career trajectory. In today's digital age, your personal brand isn't just an option – it's your career lifeline. And nowhere is this more evident than on LinkedIn.

Your personal brand is the unique combination of skills, experiences, and personality that you want the world to see. It's your professional story, told your way. On LinkedIn, your personal brand is your ticket to standing out, unlocking new opportunities, and showcasing your expertise. But here's where many professionals stumble: They wait. They wait for recognition, for opportunities, for someone to give them permission to shine. Or unfortunately they wait until they are laid off. That's where the "Promote Your Damn Self" movement comes in.

Promote Your D@mn Self isn't about bragging. It's about taking control of your narrative, confidently showcasing your skills and unique value proposition.

On LinkedIn, your personal brand isn't just a profile, it's:
- **Instant credibility:** Build a digital brand that opens doors before you knock
- **Unlimited opportunity:** Share insights that make dream jobs and clients chase you down
- **Unstoppable momentum:** Build a network that catapults you past the competition

In your career, your personal brand means taking control:
- **Shatter the glass ceiling and build your own skyscraper:** Become the CEO of your own destiny, no corner office required
- **Bulletproofing your future:** Create a personal brand so powerful, recessions become irrelevant
- **Achieving the 'impossible':** Take the wheel and drive your career to places others only dream of

Why is this crucial? Invisibility is a career killer. If you're not promoting yourself, you're letting others define your narrative—or worse, you're not even in the conversation. How often have you watched a less-skilled colleague get promoted or seen an industry newcomer rise to 'thought leader' while you remain unnoticed? You're not alone. A Gallup poll shows 70% of professionals feel they're not reaching their full potential, often due to an inability to effectively showcase their talents.

I am not gonna lie, promoting yourself isn't easy. It goes against everything we've been taught about modesty and humility. You might worry about coming across as arrogant or self-centered. Maybe you're plagued by imposter syndrome, or perhaps you're simply overwhelmed, unsure where to start.

But promoting yourself shouldn't be so difficult, and I'm here to make it easy for you. LinkedIn is the preferred platform to grow your influence, career, business, and personal brand. With over a billion users worldwide, it's the digital equivalent of the world's largest business conference, happening 24/7.

I've been where you are. For years, I watched others with half my talent getting all the glory – promotions, speaking opportunities, industry awards. Meanwhile, I was just... there. In the background. It was eating me up inside.

Finally, I couldn't take it anymore. I decided, "Forget this, I'm done being invisible." So there I was, looking at another measly 2-3% raise, despite knocking it out of the park. And that was it. The last straw. I decided to do something that scared the living daylights out of me: personal branding. I started building my personal brand, first internally at my job, then externally on LinkedIn.

I'm telling you, it was like watching me learn to walk. Over the past five years, I have gone from entry level sales manager to executive all while holding a side hustle as a coach and keynote speaker. I then started to build a network and personal brand outside of my 9 to 5 and my preferred tool was LinkedIn. I didn't know what I was doing, I didn't have a coach, I fumbled hard at first, but I persevered. Every post, every connection request - it's like I was taking baby steps into this whole new world. I was learning to evolve my mindset, show off what I knew, and position myself as a thought leader. This was mutually beneficial for my employer because I was learning skills that aided in the growth and revenue increases for the team that I served and was able to improve my quality of life and achieve financial freedom.

Six months in, boom! Paid speaking opportunity. Salary negotiations? I'm actually doing it. But the best part? The confidence I gained. The voice I found. I finally understood my worth.

Now, I'm a business coach and personal branding mentor, empowering others who were where I used to be. I'm telling you this because I want you to see what's possible. Maybe you're stuck in a job where no one sees how awesome you are. Maybe you're watching others get ahead while you're standing still. Maybe you want to start a business and are trying to figure out how to build your audience and personal brand.

Whatever it is, remember this: you're brilliant. You deserve to be seen. You deserve to be heard. It's time to step out of the shadows.

There's a revolution happening on LinkedIn right now, and those who know how to leverage it are reaping massive rewards. Most people are still using LinkedIn like it's 2010, making critical mistakes that cost them opportunities every day.

That's where you come in. By picking up this book, you've taken the first step towards joining the LinkedIn elite. You're about to learn the exact strategies that have helped thousands of professionals go from LinkedIn zero to hero.

In the next few chapters, I'm going to reveal:
- The "**Irresistible Influence Formula**": Learn how to position yourself so decision-makers line up to collaborate with you
- The "**#ShantelTaughtME Branding Blueprint**": Master the art of building your personal brand **THE RIGHT WAY** without raising eyebrows, even if you are currently employed
- The "**Hidden Goldmine Method**": Uncover your most lucrative skills that you've been overlooking

- The "**Viral Visibility Accelerator**": Discover the secret technique that turns your posts into must-read content
- The "**Authenticity over Acceptance Mindset**": Unlock powerful strategies to boost your self-assurance and command respect

Throughout this book, you'll discover how to craft a LinkedIn profile that acts as your 24/7 personal brand ambassador, how to monetize your expertise, build a high-quality network, get headhunted by top companies, and position yourself as a thought leader.

Each chapter ends with actionable steps you can take immediately to start seeing results. By the time you finish this book, you won't just have learned about LinkedIn strategy – you'll have implemented it.

You have something valuable to offer. Your experiences, your insights, your unique perspective—they matter. They matter even if you've never shared them before. And in a world hungry for authenticity and expertise, hiding your light isn't just a disservice to yourself. It's a disservice to all those who could benefit from what you have to share.

So if you're tired of being overlooked, if you're ready to step into the spotlight but unsure how, if you want to be that "it girl or it guy" but don't know where to start—you're in the right place. This book is your roadmap to LinkedIn mastery and personal brand brilliance. It's time to overcome your fears, silence your inner critic, and Promote Your D@mn Self. Because if you don't tell your story, who will?

I've been there - relocating for jobs, restarting my career, questioning myself, and even returning to school for an MBA, only to take an entry-level role after holding leadership positions at F500 companies. I've felt the sting of a first-time manager telling me I'd NEVER be in leadership. I've ridden that rollercoaster of self-doubt, and let me tell you, it's one hell of a ride.

Wake up and smell the opportunity, because the reality is this: if you wanted to promote yourself to CEO right now, this very second as you're reading these words, you absolutely can. That's exactly what I did. I became CEO in 2019 and started my very first company - a six-figure real estate business. My focus was on making more money so I needed to get promoted at work. I maintained the same budget that I had when I was only making $40K in salary. I saved my money feverishly, paid off my mortgage in less than 5 years, and turned that home into my first real estate investment property. I did this while holding down my 9 to 5.

And I'm not alone. According to a study by Guidant Financial, about 23% of small business owners were previously executives or managers before starting their own companies. That's nearly a quarter of entrepreneurs who decided to take control of their own destinies.

It may not be real estate for you but I will teach you a few ways to give yourself a pay raise and monetize your expertise and career.

Because here's the thing: you have something valuable to offer. Your experiences, your insights, your unique perspective—they matter. They matter even if you've never shared them before. Where in an era where people values realness and respect skills, concealing your abilities is more than self-limiting—it's a missed opportunity for those who could learn from you.

Friend, I hear you. It's tough feeling like you're on the sidelines when you know you've got so much to offer. But let me tell you something - you don't need to be the loudest voice in the room to make an impact.

What if, instead of chasing the spotlight, we focused on building genuine connections? Your unique experiences and perspective are valuable just as they are. Maybe it's about finding the right people who appreciate what you bring to the table.

Instead of promoting yourself, why not share your knowledge in a way that helps others? When you contribute value, people naturally take notice. It's not about becoming an "it" person, but about being authentically you.

Your worth isn't determined by likes or follows. It's in the lives you touch, the problems you solve, and the positive change you create - however small it may seem.

It's time to stop waiting for someone else to change your life, your business, your career. Be the change you want to see. The power is in your hands. You've got skills, experiences, and insights that are uniquely yours. It's time to own them, showcase them, and yes, promote them, even if you are scared.

Promote Your D@mn Self isn't just some catchy title that I made up. It's an empowerment anthem. It's me grabbing you by the shoulders and saying, "Hey, you've got something incredible to offer. Don't you dare keep it to yourself!"

As a Black woman, a mother, an executive, and an entrepreneur, I'm standing at an intersection that gives me a view like no other. And let me tell you, the view from here? It's eye-opening. I've got insights that you need to hear, and I'm not holding back. I'm giving you everything I wish someone had taught me when I was starting out.

Promote Your D@mn Self isn't about going at it alone. Trust me, I've been down that road, and it's a tough one. That is exactly why I created the Promote Your D@mn Self Group on LinkedIn. Head over and join. It's about creating a support system that cheers you on as you grow.

As we go on this journey together things will get real really fast. I've been where you are right now. I know about that voice that keeps winning an Olympic gold medal in the category of "keeping you stuck". Yeah, we're gonna kick it to the curb.

KPMG did a study that revealed that about 75% of executive women report experiencing imposter syndrome at some point in their careers. And let me tell you, it's not just the ladies - plenty of guys feel it too. No one tells you that confidence is a skill that you can learn and master.

We're gonna rewire your brain for success. I'll show you a few techniques that'll make you feel like a million dollars in 60 seconds flat. And get this - we'll turn those so-called "flaws" into your secret weapons. By the time we're done, you'll be strutting your digital stuff like you own the place. Because guess what? You do.

For those of you looking to build a personal brand while in your 9 to 5, I got you! We will talk about how to build your personal brand without putting your job at risk or upsetting your boss. I know you may be worried about your boss finding out about you building a personal on LinkedIn and thinking you're job hunting. Breathe easy, my friend. I've got you covered.

I'll teach you this strategy for updating your profile without setting off alarm bells. And I will share strategies on how to have a personal branding conversation with your boss. No sucking up required, I promise.

We're also going to craft this "Personal Brand Cocktail" - it's one part skills, two parts personality, with a twist of authenticity. Trust me, it's gonna be so tasty, people will be lining up to connect faster than free coffee at Starbucks.

I can hear you thinking, "But I'm not an expert! What could I possibly say?" Stay with me, because you're about to stand out in your field.

According to HubSpot, content creation on LinkedIn can drive 277% more effectiveness in lead generation. And you don't need to reinvent the wheel to stand out. I'll show you this method for turning everyday experiences into golden insights. By the end of this book, you'll be sharing insights so valuable and timely, your network will wonder if you've got an inside track to LinkedIn's top strategists.

We're living in a capitalist society, and your skills are more than just bullet points on a resume - they're goldmines waiting to be tapped. Every capability you've honed, every problem you've solved, every insight you've gained is a potential revenue stream. Your skills are gold mines not just on LinkedIn but in your career. You may have been the person that fixed the office printer and everyone treated you like a tech expert? Well, my friend, it's time to cash in on those skills.

Here's a mind-bender for you: according to Kinsta, about 49% of LinkedIn users earn more than $75k per year. But what they don't tell you is that many of them are making that money from side hustles they've landed through LinkedIn.

We'll go over your experience to uncover your most marketable talents - including those you've been undervaluing all along. You'd be amazed at how many skills you've mastered that others are eager to learn. Whether it's your knack for simplifying complex ideas, your ability to mediate conflicts, or your talent for spotting trends before they hit the mainstream, these are gold mines waiting to be tapped.

Confession time. How many times have you posted something on LinkedIn only to hear crickets? Yeah, we've all been there. But not anymore, my friend.

Buffer reports that LinkedIn posts with images get 2x higher engagement. But here's what no one tells you: it's not just about what you post, it's about how you hook them in.

I'll teach you this **L.E.A.D. method** that'll make thumbs freeze mid-swipe. By the time you flip that last page, you'll be looking at LinkedIn with brand new eyes. You'll see opportunities where you once saw a boring job board. You'll be ready to dive in and start making waves.

So, grab a coffee (or a wine, I won't judge), get comfy, and let's unlock this treasure chest of personal branding wisdom together. Trust me, your future self is going to be high-fiving you for this! I know you can't see me, but I'm dancing in my seat because I'm so proud of you for taking the first step in your personal branding and LinkedIn journey.

To get you ready for this journey, I've taken inventory of all the mistakes I've made and those of my clients to ensure you avoid the bumps and bruises I experienced along the way. This book is for you! Even if you've never used LinkedIn before.

Let me introduce myself. I'm Shantel Love, your personal branding mentor and I'm here to reveal a game-changing truth: your unique story is your greatest professional asset. But are you using it to its full potential?

I help ambitious professionals, especially those who've been labeled as the 'only' or 'first' in their fields, transform their LinkedIn presence into a powerful personal brand. Imagine turning your experiences of being 'othered' into your greatest strength, opening doors you never thought possible.

Curious about how I've trained thousands worldwide to win when the system wasn't made for them? My methods have led to keynote speaking opportunities, podcast appearances, and even five-figure speaking offers - all through strategic personal branding on LinkedIn.

What if you could achieve similar results without constant posting or risking your current job? What if your LinkedIn profile could attract opportunities instead of you chasing them?

If you're tired of being overlooked and ready to stand out authentically, you're in the right place. But don't take my word for it. Here's what others are saying:

"After being part of the 'Promote Your Damn Self' community and receiving coaching from Shantel, I knew I had to read her book. As an introverted marketer, I had always been content with going along to get along in my career. That all changed when I was laid off. Taking Shantel's advice, I finally 'Promoted My Damn Self.' The results were remarkable: I landed a new role with a +35% pay increase and secured $500K in sponsorship for my new project. Shantel is not only incredibly knowledgeable but also easy to talk to. Her guidance was invaluable in transforming my career."

Monica G- *Events Coordinator*- Education Technology Industry

Ready to unlock the secrets of LinkedIn mastery and personal brand brilliance? Your journey to becoming a recognized expert starts here. If you're intrigued by the power of community and the potential of your unique story, keep reading. Let's do this!

Shantel xoxo

PROMOTE YOUR D@MN SELF: BECAUSE NO ONE ELSE WILL DO IT FOR YOU

It All Starts with you

# hat you will learn

Promote Your D@mn Self isn't just advice—it's your ticket out of obscurity and into the spotlight where you belong. Curious how the "invisible" become indispensable? How the "overlooked" become in-demand? That's exactly what we're going to explore in inside these pages.

PROMOTE YOUR D@MN SELF: BECAUSE NO ONE ELSE WILL DO IT FOR YOU

You've been grinding away, day in and day out, thinking your work will speak for itself. But here's the hard truth that nobody's talking about: in today's cutthroat world, silence is career suicide. Did you know that employees who master the art of self-advocacy are 54% more likely to be satisfied with their careers? Or that those brave souls who negotiate their salaries walk away with an extra $5,000 a year on average? But here's the thing- only 37% of us are actually doing it.

It's time to stop leaving your future in someone else's hands. As my girl Caroline Ceniza-Levine puts it, "The most powerful force in your career isn't your boss, your company, or the economy. It's you and your ability to speak up for yourself." In the realm of professional development, few concepts are as transformative as personal branding. So what is a personal brand? It's the unique

> **EMPLOYEES WHO MASTER THE ART OF SELF-ADVOCACY ARE 54% MORE LIKELY TO BE SATISFIED WITH THEIR CAREERS?**

blend of your skills, experiences, and personality that you present to the world. It's your story, told through your actions, words, and attitudes, shaping how others perceive you in the professional landscape.

As we delve into the psychology behind personal branding, we encounter the self-presentation theory. This concept illuminates why personal branding is not just beneficial, but essential in today's competitive job market. The theory posits that individuals consciously attempt to influence others' perceptions of them. In the context of personal branding, this isn't about deception or manipulation; rather, it's about strategically showcasing your authentic self in the most compelling light.

Now, close your eyes for a sec and imagine this with me. Your phone buzzes – it's LinkedIn. You open it up, expecting the usual "congrats on your work anniversary" noise, but nope. It's a message from that company you've always dreamed of working with. They want you to give a talk. Forty minutes of your wisdom, your experience, your unique take on the industry you've been pouring your heart into for years.

They're not just asking. They're offering to fly you out, put you up in an expensive hotel, wine and dine you, and oh yeah, pay you a fee that makes your eyebrows shoot up so high they nearly leave your face. All for you to stand on stage and share your thought leadership. Sounds crazy, right? But here's the thing– it's not. This isn't some pie-in-the-sky fantasy. This is what happens when you step into your power as a thought leader on LinkedIn. And trust me, I've seen it happen more times than I can count in my 20 years of helping professionals just like you stand out.

But wait, there's more. After you knock that speech out of the park – because of course you do – the floodgates open. Suddenly, you're being invited back for another opportunities, this time with an even bigger paycheck. Your inbox is blowing up with new client requests. And then, the cherry on top: a headhunter slides into your DMs with a job offer that makes your jaw drop. Double your current salary. Two levels up. Fully remote.

Here's the thing, my friend. You've got the goods. You've been hustling, learning, growing, and becoming an expert in your field. But if you're not showcasing that expertise on LinkedIn and at work, you're like the proverbial tree falling in the forest with no one around to hear it. You make a noise, sure, but does it make an impact?

> **IF YOU'RE NOT SHOWCASING THAT EXPERTISE ON LINKEDIN AND AT WORK, YOU'RE LIKE THE PROVERBIAL TREE FALLING IN THE FOREST WITH NO ONE AROUND TO HEAR IT.**

I get it. Maybe you're thinking, "But I'm not a thought leader. I just do my job." Let me stop you right there. If you've been in your industry for any length of time, you've got insights that others need to hear. Whether you've been in customer service for a few years, leading teams for many years, or solving complex problems day in and day out, you've built up a wealth of knowledge that's uniquely yours.

Even the powerful business leaders, the C-suite execs I work with, struggle with this sometimes. They can run multimillion-dollar companies but balk at the idea of positioning themselves as thought leaders. Imposter syndrome is real, and it doesn't discriminate based on job title.

But here's the secret: Thought leadership isn't about being the smartest person in the room. It's about being willing to share your perspective, to start conversations, to add value to your network. And LinkedIn? It's your stage, your megaphone, your personal branding HQ all rolled into one.

With over a billion users, LinkedIn is where decisions are made, careers are launched, and thought leaders are born. Your profile isn't just a digital resume – it's the landing page for (Insert Your Name) Brand. It's where hiring managers, potential clients, investors, and life-changing opportunities come to learn about what you bring to the table.

So, are you ready to step into the spotlight? To turn your expertise into opportunities? To become the go-to person in your field? Because let me tell you, the world is ready for what you have to offer. And by the time we're done here, you'll not only see the thought leader in yourself, but you'll have the tools to show the world too.

This is the future I see for you. Promotions that catapult your income. High-paying clients and speaking opportunities falling into your lap. You are established as the influential thought leader you truly are. Your brilliance making waves, your goals within easy reach, and the success you've always deserved is finally yours for the taking. You just have to commit to doing the work.

I'm Shantel Love, the brains behind Promote Your Damn Self. Consider me your personal hype woman and mentor, here to show you how to increase your confidence and influence by building an outstanding personal brand, and leverage LinkedIn as your secret weapon.

I'm about to spill all the tea – the exact strategies and frameworks my clients invest thousands for in one-on-one coaching. No holding back, no smoke and mirrors – just straight-up, no-gatekeeping advice on how to build your personal brand, your way.

Whether you're an experienced professional, an up-and-coming entrepreneur, or just someone looking for a career boost, this book's got your name on it. It's your roadmap to turning your experience into a brand and LinkedIn profile into a magnet for opportunities – we're talking learning and development opportunities, job offers, speaking opportunities, podcast invites, you name it.

Let's get real for a second. As I'm writing this, over 83,000 workers in the US have been shown the door by tech companies alone. It's a gut-punch of a number, and it hits close to home. I've seen friends and colleagues who gave their all to a company suddenly treated like yesterday's news.

I've been there too. Back in 2010, I got the boot despite making millions for my employer and saving them even more. They had the nerve to offer me a lower position with less pay to stick around. Talk about a wake-up call. But you know what? It lit a fire under me. That was the day my personal brand journey kicked off.

After that, I went into full reinvention mode. Started multiple businesses, climbed from entry-level sales to exec in five years flat, and found my calling in empowering professionals like you to navigate similar choppy waters. I've also learned a lot and made a lot of mistakes so that you don't have to. Promote Your D@mn Self isn't just a book – it's my mission to empower you to take control over your career, your life, your personal brand, and crank up the volume on your voice.

I see it this way: a personal brand is like career insurance. It's not about showing off; it's about making sure your worth and achievements are front and center, come hell or high water.

Before I embraced the Promote Your D@mn Self mindset, I was right where many of my clients started. Hiding behind my keyboard, taking thankless speaking opportunities, watching promotions pass me by. I sold myself short with cheap coaching offers and kept my mouth shut about my achievements because I thought that's what I was supposed to do.

Sound familiar? Maybe you've been told to wait your turn, change who you are, or jump through more hoops to prove yourself. Maybe you've been told to keep quiet about your wins and play it safe.

Well, let me tell you – that's not what Promote Your D@mn Self is about.

I've thrown myself into learning, hired coaches, devoured books, and spent more money than I care to admit, all searching for answers. My personal branding journey led to my first podcast opportunity through a LinkedIn connection – the reward? A water bottle and a t-shirt (insert side eye). But it was enough to light the spark. With my husband cheering me on, I found my calling in helping others turn their passion into profit.

The revelation hit me like a bolt of lightning: while my corporate job offered valuable lessons and steady income, it alone wasn't the key to financial freedom. I realized that true economic empowerment comes from leveraging these experiences—the rich resources of knowledge, connections, and opportunities—for long-term investment and success. Energized by this economic awakening, I couldn't help but imagine the impact of sharing this revelation. It became clear that my mission was to teach others how to harness their careers as powerful tools in their journey to true financial independence.

This realization sparked a passion for empowering others. Through my workshops, coaching, and speaking engagements, I've witnessed firsthand how embracing one's experience can transform careers and lives. We've cultivated an vibrant community on LinkedIn where professionals like you can confront the fear of personal branding head-on and build the confidence to pursue your dreams. Together, we're redefining success and paving the way for a new generation of empowered, passionate entrepreneurs.

Join our Promote Your D@mn Self LinkedIn Group here:
https://www.linkedin.com/groups/14464148/.

You don't have to go it alone. We are in this together.

I get it – building a personal brand can feel like climbing Everest in flip-flops. You might be worried about coming off as a show-off on LinkedIn or freaking out about your boss seeing your posts. Maybe you're feeling stuck in your career, passed over for promotions, or just plain lost on where to start with this whole personal branding thing.

Trust me, I've been in those shoes. I know the frustration of feeling undervalued and the overwhelm of trying to figure out how to build a personal brand and leverage LinkedIn. But here's the secret – you don't need a gazillion followers or a fancy C-suite title to get started. Everyone starts somewhere, and I'm here to show you how to work your unique magic from day one.

This book isn't just theory pulled out of thin air – it's battle-tested strategies. I've weathered layoffs, climbed from the bottom rung to the executive suite, and launched businesses that actually make money, all using the strategies I'm about to share with you.

And if you've never heard of personal branding, so much as hit 'post' on LinkedIn, been a guest on a podcast, or even thought about calling yourself a thought leader, don't worry. The Promote Your D@mn Self framework has helped clients go from zero to launching businesses, charging top dollar for coaching, and landing speaking opportunities while holding down a 9 to 5 – even without a lick of previous experience.

This isn't about waiting your turn or playing by outdated rules. It's about writing and living your story, stepping into your spotlight, and declaring your worth loud and proud. It's about being unapologetically you and using that to build a personal brand that turns heads and opens doors.

Maybe you grabbed this book because you're low-key terrified of taking that first step on LinkedIn. You're sweating bullets thinking about your boss stumbling across your posts, worried it might jeopardize your current opportunity or future prospects.

Or perhaps you're that high-performing employee, consistently crushing it, yet somehow always left in the dust when it comes to promotions and pay bumps. You're watching others climb the ladder while you're stuck wondering what secret sauce you're missing. Maybe you're killing it in your business, but when it comes to tooting your own horn? Crickets. You're at a total loss on how to even start building your personal brand.

You might look at LinkedIn and see nothing but a cesspool of humble brags and corporate goodie two shoes—too phony or self-important for your taste.

But let's be real, deep down you're hungry for more. You dream of being that go-to expert, dropping knowledge bombs on podcasts, and inspiring crowds from center stage. You want clients beating down your door, drawn in by your skills and genuine vibe.

Yet despite your hustle, you feel like you're shouting into the black hole. You're trying to market yourself, but it's like no one's got their ears on. You want to recognized and rewarded for your efforts at work. You're stumped on what to say, how to say it, and where to even begin. The struggle to land job promotions/offers, attract clients, or even get a few measly followers? It's all too real and overwhelming.

If any of this hits home, take a breath—you've landed in the right spot. You're not alone in this personal branding journey. In fact, by owning up to these challenges, you're already miles ahead of others just starting out.

As we take on this adventure together, I'm gonna hit you with some real, actionable steps at the end of each chapter—concrete moves designed to get you closer to your goals.

I'm all about that "action equals results" life, so every chapter wraps up with a ta-da list (because we don't just say, to do because we are about make magic… ta-da!) tailored to get you where you wanna be.

I'm serious about seeing you win. I've witnessed firsthand how a mindset overhaul can flip careers and lives on their head. In Promote Your D@mn Self, we're all about that Authenticity over Acceptance Mindset. It's about showcasing the real you and your values, not chasing likes or morphing into what others expect. We know how exhausting it is to code-switch and wear a mask someone else made for you. We've also seen the relief that happens when you reclaim your authentic self.

To build the personal brand or life you're thirsting for, you might need to rewire your brain a bit. The first chapter tackles those irritating fears about putting yourself out there on LinkedIn.

YESTERDAY'S LINKEDIN IS NOT TODAY'S LINKEDIN

You know what? It's mind-blowing how LinkedIn has totally transformed over the years. Remember when we first started using it? Goodness, it was basically just an online resume, right? I used to live on LinkedIn as a recruiter, building teams across all sorts of industries. It was great for keeping tabs on work milestones and sharing the occasional promotion, but that was about it.

Let me tell you a story about the power of LinkedIn, even back in the day. Get this, I'm in Redwood City, California, crunching numbers doing accounting work at a software company. Sure, I'm doing the job, but let me tell you, I'm not feeling it. At all. Here I am, in my early twenties, a Detroit girl transplanted to the West Coast, no friends or family in sight just trying to get my money's worth from this degree before Sallie Mae comes asking me to pay her back. Oh, and my boss? Never even met the lady face-to-face. I'm pulling in decent income for my age, but fulfillment? That's nowhere to be found.

So there I am, getting ready to give this important presentation to the big bosses. I've prepped for hours, days, weeks. I walk into that boardroom, decked out in my white ruffled blouse, navy pencil skirt, and these bright yellow pumps. I'm all set – laptop plugged in, spreadsheets ready, greeting everyone cool as a collected.

Then, bam! The universe throws me a curveball. Mid-presentation, I notice this vase on the table doing the cha-cha slide, and suddenly the whole room starts shaking like crazy. My heart's pounding out of my chest. It's my first earthquake, and this Midwest girl is not having it. I grab my purse and make a beeline for the exit. I'm halfway down the hall when one of the leaders chases after me, asking where I'm off to. "I'm going home," I tell him. Right then and there, I realized that I hated accounting. And accepted that earthquakes and I are never going to be friends.

This was the turning point in my life. I dust off my networking and recruiting skills and hit up LinkedIn like it's my job. I spot an opening at a place where a friend of a friend works. So I reach out, asking if they can put in a good word for me.

Next thing I know, I'm at the top of the candidate list. I ace the interview the following week, and before I can say "see ya later, earthquakes," I'm packing my bags for Minnesota to lead contact centers in telecom. This journey – from nearly getting shaken out of my pumps to landing a job that I love closer to home – taught me two things: resilience and your network, are your secret weapons? That's your key to success.

Fast forward to now, and it's a whole different ballgame. LinkedIn's become this massive global network with over a billion users. Can you believe it? It's like the Facebook of the professional world, sitting pretty as the sixth most popular social platform out there.

The numbers are mind-blowing. Nearly 80% of recruiters are on there constantly, and get this – over 60 million people are job hunting on LinkedIn every single week. That's insane!

But here's the thing – LinkedIn isn't just about job searching anymore. It's become this incredible stage for your personal brand. Think about it: you can showcase your expertise, connect with people who are passionate about the same stuff you are, and really establish yourself as a go-to person in your field.

Did you know that 94% of B2B marketers are using LinkedIn to share content? It's not just a job board anymore – it's your stage to build a community, make your voice heard, and shake things up in your industry.

Here's something that always sticks with me: Jeff Bezos once said, "Your brand is what other people say about you when you're not in the room." LinkedIn? It's your chance to control that narrative.

Think about the people you look up to on LinkedIn. What makes them stand out? It's not just their fancy titles or achievements. It's their realness, their willingness to share the highs and the lows. That's what builds trust and makes people want to connect with them.

Take Caroline Wanga, for example. She went from intern to Chief Diversity and Inclusion Officer at Target, and now she's the CEO of Essence Communications. She uses LinkedIn like a boss, sharing her non-traditional career path and the challenges she faced as a Black woman in corporate America. Her authenticity is her superpower. Go check her out and tell her Shantel Love sent you.

So, how can you use LinkedIn to build your own powerful personal brand?

Think about what makes you, well, YOU. Your journey, your experiences, your expertise – that's the gold. How can you showcase that on LinkedIn to open doors and get noticed?

Imagine logging in and seeing a profile that screams 'you'. A headline that grabs attention, a summary that captures your essence, and an experience section that tells your growth story. Picture recruiters or potential clients stumbling on your page and thinking, "Damn, I need to talk to this person."

Now, imagine sharing content that makes people stop scrolling. Articles, posts, videos – whatever your mind creates. Each piece positions you as someone who knows their stuff. Picture your ideas reaching thousands of professionals who can't wait to hear what you'll say next.

Think about connecting with the experts in your industry. LinkedIn is your ticket to building relationships that could lead to game-changing opportunities. Picture yourself confidently jumping into discussions and adding value to your network. Remember, on LinkedIn, you're not just your job title. You're the sum of all your experiences and what makes you unique. It's not about who you know, but who you can connect with.

I've seen people with no fancy titles make incredible connections with top execs at huge companies. How? They had the guts to reach out and ask for that connection. Think about that. They dared to knock on a virtual door that seemed out of reach, and it opened up a world of possibilities.

Isn't it amazing how LinkedIn can make these opportunities happen? You can connect with anyone – executives, industry leaders, potential clients, future employers – all with a simple click.

Let me share my one click experience with you. In the tech industry, success can be a lonely affair. As a woman of color who had climbed to the role of VP, I found myself yearning for connection and representation. That's when I stumbled upon a podcast featuring a Latina CTO, a member of the LGBTQ+ community, whose words resonated deeply with my own experiences.

Driven by curiosity and a willingness to embrace potential rejection, I reached out. To my surprise, she responded, and we soon found ourselves in a virtual conversation that felt as intimate as old friends catching up. Her advice was simple yet powerful: build your personal brand, advocate for yourself, and don't shy away from opportunities that scare you.

Little did I know that this chance connection would become a catalyst for transformation. Inspired by her TEDx talk on mentoring women and her company's mission to create opportunities for minorities in tech, I began to see the true potential of my own voice and experiences.

What followed was a whirlwind of growth and recognition. I became a respected thought leader in Customer Success, collecting awards, featuring on podcasts, and speaking at high-profile events. But the real victory wasn't in the accolades – it was in the opportunity to mentor and inspire others, just as I had been inspired.

This journey taught me the immense power of paying it forward and breaking down gates. By taking a calculated risk and reaching out to a stranger, I not only changed the trajectory of my own career but also gained the ability to impact countless others. In the end, I learned that true success isn't measured by how high we climb, but by how many people we lift up along the way.

Think about what LinkedIn could do for you - whether you're climbing the corporate ladder, running your own business, or switching careers. I've seen people in my circle and those I've coached go from invisible on LinkedIn making connections to landing their first paid client in just a month.

One of my clients spoke about doing just that, here is what Muhammad had to say:

> I'm a web designer who recently faced a tough time. Two months passed without finding any clients, and I started losing confidence in my skills. That's when Shantel Love came into the picture as my coach. Shantel's guidance was like a beacon of light during my difficult phase. She not only mentored me but also helped me rediscover my strengths and regain my confidence. With her encouragement and practical advice, I tackled the challenges head-on. The results were incredible! Under Shantel's mentorship, I started three new website creation projects and

secured two monthly website maintenance service contracts. This turnaround was a significant boost to my career and self-belief."

— "

You can just feel the transformation that happened in Muhammad. He is not an exception, you can have the same for you!

My clients have built networks that bring them speaking opportunities on everything from, wellness, sales growth, skill-building, career transitions, and more. And guess what? This positive outcome works even if you're a total newbie.

Building your personal brand on LinkedIn not only elevates your profile but also hones your professional skills in real-time. As you curate content, engage with industry leaders, and articulate your unique perspectives, you're constantly learning and refining your expertise. This process of continuous growth and self-promotion makes you an increasingly valuable asset to both your current employer and potential clients, positioning you as a forward-thinking, adaptable professional who's always one step ahead in your field.

Shantel's guidance was like a beacon of light during my difficult phase!

So don't sleep on LinkedIn. Embrace it, explore it, and watch it work its magic. Your success story starts with one click. If you're new to this and haven't even set up an account yet, turn the page and I will walk you through how to get started.

Connect with me on LinkedIn

If you are **NEW** to LinkedIn and haven't even created an account yet, let's change that right now. Head over to LinkedIn's sign-up page and get the ball rolling. Here is the LinkedIn sign-up link: Linkedin.com

While you're at it, *shoot me a connection request right now a*t: www.linkedin.com/in/shantellove and tell me that you are reading this book. It's all about growing your network and presence from day one. I promise I'll accept your request.

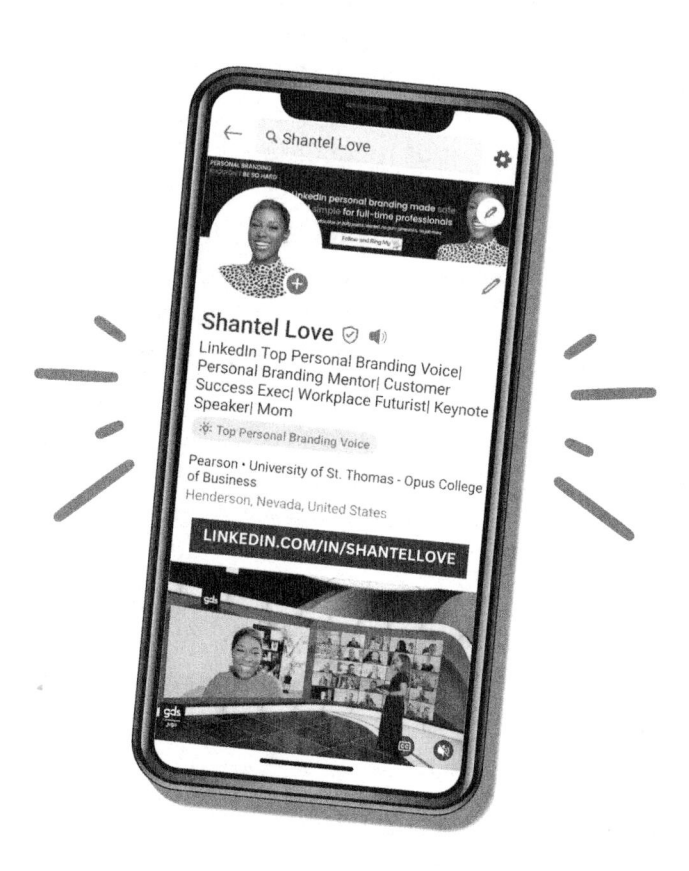

17

TAKE IT FROM SHANTEL ...

I wasn't always this confident on LinkedIn. I used to tie myself in knots worrying about stuff like:

- What if my boss sees me posting?
- Who would even listen to me?
- What the hell should I say?
- What if I pour my heart into a post and crickets... no likes, no comments, nada?

I've been there, done that with all these feelings. And let me tell you, you're not alone. But here's the thing—I know you're a pro. Better yet, I know you're an expert who could be landing opportunities, paid speaking opportunities, promotions, and big-money contracts with corporate clients.

If you are still thinking, "why should I care about my personal brand"? When it comes to personal branding, silence isn't humility—it's invisibility. Your personal brand on LinkedIn isn't bragging; it's your professional lifeline. By mastering the concept shared in Promote Your D@mn Self, you're not just showcasing your skills—you're opening doors, attracting opportunities, and future-proofing your career. Remember, if you don't tell your story and highlight your value, no one else will.

If you've been hiding in the shadows with all your talent and no one knows who you are, don't worry. We're going to work through these limiting beliefs and show you how to protect yourself while avoiding putting your job at risk.

Sounds good? I heard that "YEEEEESSSSS (with a lot of S's)," keep reading.

THINGS TO REMEMBER FROM THIS CHAPTER

Promote Your D@mn Self: Because No One Else Will Do It For You:

- Your brilliance and hard work mean nothing if they're invisible. Your achievements may not always speak for themselves—you need to be their voice.
- Promoting yourself isn't arrogance, it's survival in today's career jungle. You're not just tooting your own horn; you're ensuring your value is recognized and rewarded. No one else has as much invested in your success as you do, so waiting for others to champion you is a losing strategy.

LinkedIn's Evolution

- LinkedIn has transformed from a simple online resume to a powerful platform for personal branding and networking.

Reflect on how you've been using LinkedIn. Are you still treating it like just a digital resume/CV? It's time to shift your perspective and start leveraging its full potential.

The Power of Personal Stories

Your experiences, even the challenging ones, can become powerful tools for connection and growth on LinkedIn. Your experiences, even the challenging ones, can become powerful tools for connection and growth on LinkedIn. You might feel a

THINGS TO REMEMBER FROM THIS CHAPTER

ping of anxiety or resistance at the thought of sharing – that's normal, but pushing through that discomfort is where the real growth happens.

I'm here to support you. I have an exercise for you that will encourage you to take action.

Let's take action Step up and share on LinkedIn that you're reading "Promote Your D@mn Self". Don't just consume - put these lessons into practice right now. What's the most powerful insight you've gained so far? Share it boldly.

Remember, vulnerability isn't weakness - it's your secret weapon. It's what makes you relatable and real in a sea of polished profiles. By opening up, you're not just promoting yourself, you're connecting authentically.

This isn't just an exercise - it's your first step towards mastering your personal brand. You're showing the world you're someone who takes action, who's coachable, who's ready to stand out.

We often fall into the trap of passive learning, but true growth comes from applying what you learn. It's time to move from knowledge to mastery. By sharing your journey with "Promote Your D@mn Self", you're not just reading a book - you're actively building your brand.

So go ahead, make that post. Let your network see the emerging expert you are.

THINGS TO REMEMBER FROM THIS CHAPTER

Networking and Opportunities

LinkedIn is a global networking party where every connection could lead to a life-changing opportunity. You might think, "I'm not good at networking" or "I don't have anything impressive to share," but remember: authentic connections aren't about being perfect or extraordinary – they're about being genuinely you and sharing your real experiences.

Let's take action: Reach out to someone in your industry you admire. Send them a thoughtful message explaining why you'd like to connect. We don't do stuck here so, here's a template to get you going.

Temple: Connecting with a Fellow [Industry] Professional

Hi [Name],

I hope this message finds you well. My name is [Your Name], and I'm a [Your Role] at [Your Company/Organization]. I've been following your work in [specific area or project] and have been truly inspired by [specific reason—e.g., your innovative approach, your leadership, etc.].

I would love to connect and learn more about your experiences in [industry/field]. I believe that exchanging insights could be mutually beneficial, and I'd be grateful for the opportunity to hear your thoughts on [specific topic or shared interest].

THINGS TO REMEMBER FROM THIS CHAPTER

Thank you for considering my request. I look forward to the possibility of connecting.
Best,

[Your Name]
[Your LinkedIn Profile or Contact Information]

Once your a done message me and let me know how it went!

Let's take action:

Head over to the Promote Your D@mn Self community on LinkedIn and start by connecting with at least three new members.

Join the group by following this link:

https://www.linkedin.com/groups/14464148/.

Introduce yourself with a personalized message, highlighting what drew you to the community and what you hope to gain from it. Engage with their posts and share your insights to foster meaningful interactions. This is a secret to growing. Turning strangers to friends.

Remember, your journey on LinkedIn is unique to you. Embrace your story, share your expertise, and don't be afraid to **Promote Your D@mn Self** on LinkedIn. The opportunities are waiting - you just need to take that first step.

> "YOUR PERSONAL BRAND ISN'T JUST WHAT YOU SAY; IT'S WHAT YOU DO, HOW YOU MAKE PEOPLE FEEL, AND THE LEGACY YOU LEAVE BEHIND"

Shantel Love

YOUR NOTES:

Take a moment to reflect

YOUR NOTES:

Take a moment to reflect

YOUR NOTES:

Take a moment to reflect

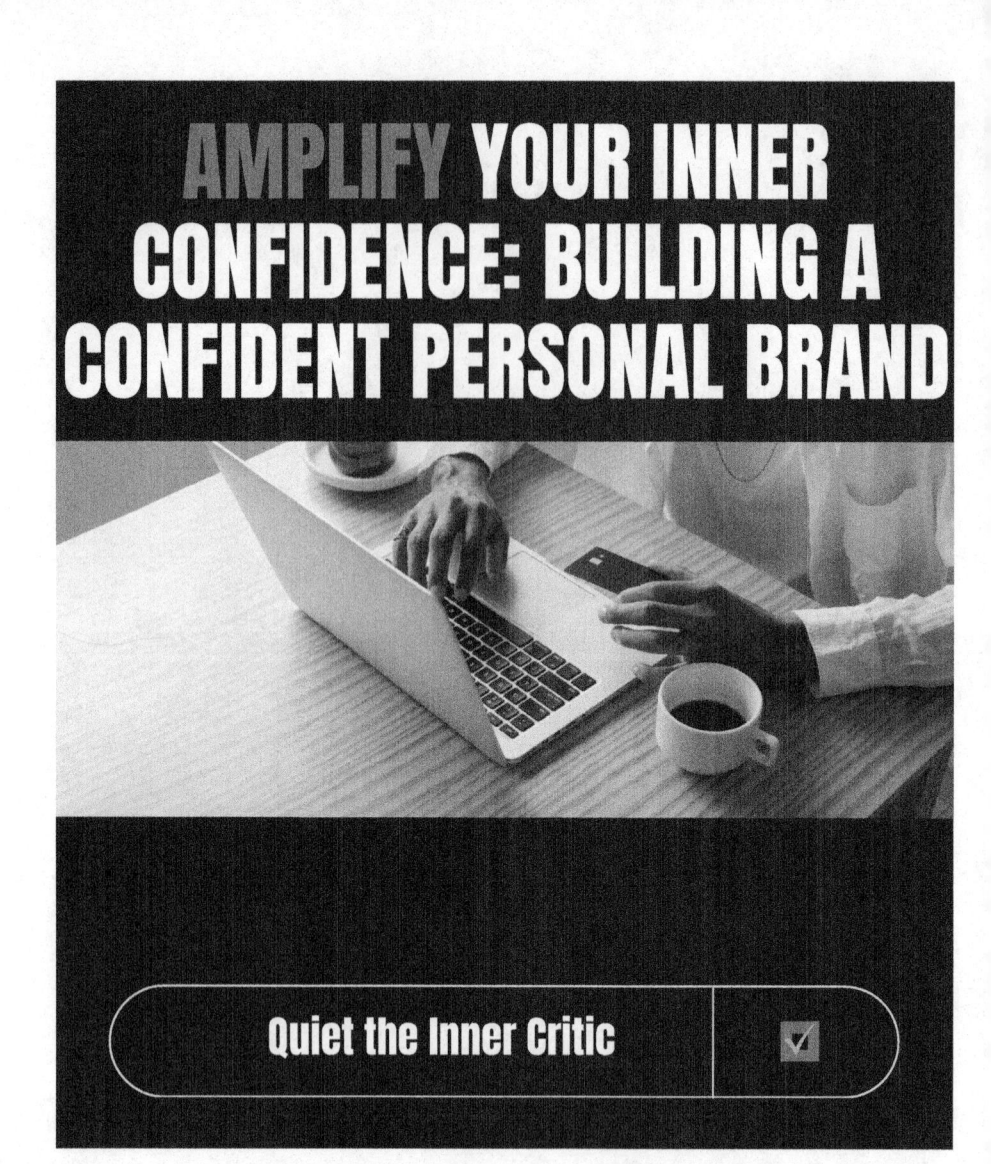

AMPLIFY YOUR INNER CONFIDENCE: BUILDING A CONFIDENT PERSONAL BRAND

Quiet the Inner Critic ☑

What you will learn

The #1 secret to personal branding revealed: Mastering your mindset. Discover how to silence your inner critic, unleash your hidden potential, and project an unwavering confidence that will make the world sit up and take notice.

AMPLIFY YOUR INNER CONFIDENCE: BUILDING A CONFIDENT PERSONAL BRAND

"Confidence isn't about gaining others' approval; it's about thriving even if your past was tough and your beginnings were humble. True confidence is knowing you'll succeed regardless of what others think." — Shantel Love, MBA

Welcome to the Authenticity over Acceptance Revolution

I know you're ready to learn about personal branding and how to do that on LinkedIn, we will get there. I promise. We will start with confidence because everything that you want to be in life, starts with confidence and your belief system. It starts with having the confidence to believe in yourself and your ability. It starts with truly knowing yourself.

Ask yourself, "Who am I?"

Three simple words. One earth-shattering question.

Close your eyes for a moment. Take a deep breath. Now, ask yourself: Who am I, really? Not who the world thinks I am. Not who my parents, friends, or colleagues expect me to be. Who am I at my core, stripped of all pretenses and expectations?

If you're like most people, this question probably makes you uncomfortable. It might even terrify you. Because the truth is, many of us have spent so long living behind a carefully curated facade that we've lost touch with our authentic selves.

From the moment we take our first breath, the world starts telling us who we should be. Society, media, even our well-meaning families overwhelm us with messages about how to act, what to like, how to present ourselves. And slowly, falsely, we start to shape our identities around these external expectations rather than listening to the quiet voice inside that's trying to guide us towards our authentic selves.

The result? A generation living a lie about who they really are. A generation trapped in the prison of "not enough":

- Not **smart** enough.
- Not **brave** enough.
- Not **experienced** enough.
- Not **rich** enough.

What if the very things you've been told make you "not enough" are actually your greatest strengths? What if I told you that on the other side of these limitations resides a life that is so freeing? What if I told you that you have the power right now to rid yourself of those limiting beliefs?

This rebellion isn't just about "being yourself." It's about rediscovering who that self truly is. It's about peeling back layers of societal conditioning, shedding the weight of others' expectations, and embracing the raw, unfiltered essence of who you are.

Take a moment right now, to question these limitations. Are they truly barriers you've encountered, or just invisible lines you've been conditioned to believe you can't cross?

Why does this matter? Because authenticity is the bedrock of true confidence. And confidence? Well, that's the secret that turns dreams into reality, potential into achievement, and ordinary lives into extraordinary ones.

Let me ask you this. How often have you muted your brilliance to avoid outshining others? When was the last time you silenced your authentic voice, burying genuine thoughts and desires beneath a veneer of societal expectations? And as you look into the mirror, do you truly see yourself, or merely a carefully constructed facade designed to appease everyone but the person staring back at you?

If you're nodding along, congratulations. You've just taken the first step towards breaking free from what I call the "**liedentity**"— a false identity built on lies we've been told (and told ourselves) about who we should be.

This liedentity is deceptive. It whispers that you're not smart, brave, or experienced enough. It's a false narrative you've internalized, shaped by others' expectations. It's imposter syndrome invalidating your successes and magnifying your failures.

But how can you NOT be enough if you were beautifully and wonderfully made in his image?

But what if I told you that this liedentity is nothing more than a paper tiger? What if the very traits you've been hiding—your quirks, your passions, your unconventional ideas—are actually your greatest strengths?

This is where the real work begins. Uncovering your authentic self isn't a gentle stroll through the park. It's a journey, fraught with challenges, self-doubt, and moments of uncomfortable truth. But on the other side of this journey lies a version of you that's unstoppable. A **YOU** that's magnetic, influential, and unshakably confident.

Imagine for a moment:
- Walking into a room and immediately commanding attention— not because you're the loudest or the most perfectly polished, but because you radiate an unshakable sense of self.

- Pursuing your dreams without the paralyzing fear of judgment or failure, because you know your worth isn't tied to others' opinions.
- Building a personal brand so authentic and compelling that opportunities and connections naturally gravitate towards you.

This isn't just feel-good fantasy. This is the tangible, real-world power of embracing your authentic self.

This Authenticity over Acceptance Revolution isn't just about breaking glass ceilings or fitting into some predetermined mold of success. It's about shattering the entire concept of limits and rewriting the rulebook on personal branding for those of us who color outside the lines.

Your story is waiting to be written, and trust me, it's going to be one hell of a bestseller. Every insecurity, every "unconventional" experience, every moment that seemed like a detour on your journey? That's not just your past—it's your power. It's the competitive advantage that makes you irresistible in a world drowning in bland conformity.

That summer you spent waiting tables, handling even the nastiest customers with a smile? That's customer service gold. The resourcefulness you gained from growing up with limited means? That translates into masterfully managing budgets and saving companies millions. Your journey isn't a random series of events

In this Authenticity over Acceptance Revolution, the sky isn't the limit—it's just the beginning. And you, with all your glorious, unfiltered, non-"country club" experiences? You're not just part of this revolution. You're leading it.

So, are you ready for the revolution? Are you prepared to challenge every assumption you've made about who you are and who you're supposed to be?

In the following pages, we're going to embark on a transformative journey. We'll dismantle the "liedentity" piece by piece. We'll confront the fears and doubts that have held you back. And we'll rebuild your sense of self on a foundation of unshakable authenticity.

This isn't just about feeling good (although that's a fantastic side effect). This is about revolutionizing how you show up in the world. It's about creating a personal brand so genuine and powerful that it becomes your secret weapon in business, relationships, and life.

The path won't always be easy. There will be moments of discomfort, of doubt, of wanting to retreat back into the safety of your old patterns. But I promise you this: The view from the other side is worth every challenging step.

Are you ready to meet the real you? Are you prepared to unleash your authentic self and watch as the world rises to meet you?

The revolution starts now. And it starts with you.

Let me tell you about Terrence, a living, breathing example of what happens when you challenge your "liedentity" and embrace your authentic self.

Terrence had it all on paper – a voice smooth as silk and leadership skills that could make a Fortune 500 CEO jealous. His dream? To become a renowned speaker and thought leader in his industry. But despite his impressive skillset and experience, Terrence was trapped in a prison of self-doubt, his potential shackled by the lies he'd internalized about himself.
For years, Terrence had been talking the talk in corporate jobs, but when it came to real speaking opportunities, he'd go silent. It wasn't a lack of ability holding him back, it was his liedentity, that false narrative telling him he wasn't good enough, experienced

enough, or worthy enough to step into the spotlight.

This is where the power of authentic confidence comes into play. As Terrence's coach, I saw his potential clear as day. Sometimes, you need to borrow someone else's belief in you until you can cultivate your own. So I challenged him, gently but persistently, to question the lies he'd been telling himself and to take that leap of faith.

I'll never forget standing beside Terrence before his first major speech. He was visibly nervous, teetering on the edge of fight or flight. But there was no turning back. As his name was called, Terrence stepped onto that stage – and what happened next was nothing short of transformational.

In that moment, Terrence didn't just give a speech; he shed his liedentity like an old, ill-fitting skin. He owned that stage with a confidence that came from a place of authenticity, speaking with passion and connecting with his audience in a way that only happens when you're truly being yourself.

The result? Within 24 hours, Terrence was inundated with opportunities – a job offer, podcast invitations, even an all-expenses-paid speaking engagement. It was as if the universe was responding to his newfound authenticity, saying, "This is where you belong."

Terrence's story isn't just about overcoming insecurities; it's a powerful testament to what happens when you challenge your liedentity and step into your authentic power. It demonstrates that sometimes, all you need is the courage to question your self-imposed limitations and the faith to believe in your true self – even if you have to "faith it 'til you make it" for a while. This journey of authentic self-discovery isn't about "faking it" in the traditional sense. It's about having faith in your inherent worth and potential, even when your liedentity is screaming otherwise. It's about maintaining a positive mindset and resilience in the face of self-doubt and external challenges.

Now, Terrence is out there building his personal brand on LinkedIn, thriving as a thought leader and speaker. His journey from self-doubt to authentic confidence is a blueprint for what's possible when you embrace your true self, quirks, unconventional experiences, and all.

So if you're hesitating about chasing your dreams, think about Terrence. Take that leap. Challenge your liedentity. Borrow some confidence if you need to. Because in this Authenticity over Acceptance Revolution, the most powerful personal brand is the one that's genuinely, unapologetically you. And trust me, when you finally let your authentic self shine, you might just blow your own mind with what you can achieve.

So, tell me, why are you sitting there admiring others' journeys when you've got your own amazing story to tell? I know why, because I've been there too, trapped in my own "liedentity" - that false narrative we tell ourselves about who we are and what we're capable of. I used to be a master of disguise, but my toughest act was fooling myself. For years, I danced to everyone else's tune, desperately seeking approval like it was oxygen.

Have you ever felt like an outsider in your own life story? I have. Growing up in Detroit, raised by a single teenage mother, I was that wide-eyed girl staring up at skyscrapers, wondering if I'd ever reach those heights. The world seemed intent on writing my story before I could even grasp the pen, and I believed every word of that limiting liedentity.

But here's the thing about stories - they have a way of surprising you. My journey began in the shadows of those towering buildings, where poverty and societal expectations tried to box me in. I wore shame like a second skin, believing the label of "limited potential" that others had slapped on me. My liedentity told me I was a chameleon, changing colors to fit in, suffocating beneath the masks I wore.

Then came the fall. After college, I found myself homeless, sleeping in my car. My dreams seemed as distant as those skyscrapers I once admired. Rock bottom? I was digging deeper, my liedentity whispering that this was all I deserved.

But in that moment of despair, an unexpected plot twist occurred. A stranger, seeing beyond my circumstances and my liedentity, offered me shelter. This act of kindness sparked an epiphany: I am unbound by my circumstances and the false narratives I've believed about myself. Our value isn't defined by our past, present struggles, or the lies we've internalized. We are FREE to shape our future. This realization was my call to adventure, my wake-up call to challenge my liedentity.

Armed with this new perspective, I embarked on a journey to dismantle my liedentity. From homelessness to a sales role, from entry-level to executive in just five years. I founded three successful businesses. Each achievement was a testament to the power that happens when I challenged the lies I'd believed about myself. But the real transformation? That happened inside as I confronted and rewrote my liedentity.

I faced my inner critic head-on, rewiring my entire being. I granted myself permission to accept my past, own my present, and dream without limits. The game-changer? Becoming the C.E.O. of my own life. I embraced every part of myself - flaws and all - rejecting the liedentity that had held me back for so long. I celebrated every win and committed to growth, realizing authenticity and personal development go hand in hand in dismantling our liedentities.

Stepping into my full, authentic self, free from the shackles of my liedentity, unleashed a power I never knew I had. That's when my real story began. Now, I stand tall like those skyscrapers as a force of nature. I've learned that your journey, your voice, your truth - they're your superpower. No one can tell your story like you can, and no liedentity can define you unless you let it.

Remember this: you're the architect of your own journey, the author of your own story.

When I started writing this book, my inner critic – I call her Big Bertha – threw an epic tantrum. She rattled off every reason why I shouldn't do it, why I'd fail, why I'd end up hiding under a rock from embarrassment. It was like being stuck in an interrogation room with my own insecurities playing good cop, bad cop. This was my liedentity making its last stand, trying desperately to keep me small and safe.

Since we are being honest, I didn't trust myself. I rewrote this book three and a half times, each revision a battle against my liedentity. The first draft? Knocked it out in a week. The final version? Months of blood, sweat, and deleted paragraphs. I found myself in an existential tug-of-war with my "Why" – you know, that deep-rooted reason that drives us to do what we do, the authentic voice that our liedentities try to silence.

But guess what, insecurities and all: I wrote this book anyway. Not because I suddenly became fearless, but because I learned to tango with my fear and challenge my liedentity. Why do I tell you this? Because I want you to see that the power you're seeking is already within you, buried under layers of false narratives and liedentities. My story isn't unique – it's a reflection of the struggles we all face as we try to break free from our liedentities. The doubts you're feeling? I've been there. The fear of putting yourself out there? Been there too. And if I can push through it and challenge my liedentity, so can you.

I see it this way: fear and our liedentities are like that one relative who shows up to every family gathering, invited or not. Instead of trying to change the locks, you might as well hand them a plate and let them hang around. Just don't let them DJ the party or write your story. Your journey, with all its ups and downs, is what makes you uniquely you. It's time to embrace it, share it, and let it inspire others. Because in the end, it's not just about overcoming your fears and liedentities – it's about using them as stepping stones on your path to becoming the authentic, unstoppable force you were always meant to be.

I wrote this book because I've been in the trenches of personal branding, and let me tell you, it shouldn't be rocket science. They don't teach this stuff in school, and for us corporate employees, resources are scarce. Even when you're excelling, standing out can feel like screaming into the void. And those systemic roadblocks? They're real, designed to keep you "in your place."

As a Black woman in the corporate jungle, I've faced obstacles that would make advanced calculus look easy. I've climbed to the top, becoming the first Black female VP in my division's history. Often, I'm the only one who looks like me in the room.

When was the last time you saw someone who looked like you in a position you aspire to reach?

Growing up, Black women in executive leadership were unicorns. Their voices were muffled, dismissed, or caricatured. I've had nights wondering, "Am I reaching too high? Who am I to think I can change the game?" But here's the truth - I did change the game. And so can you!

My journey hasn't been easy. Maybe you're nodding along, thinking, "Preach, sister. I've got my own war stories." Or maybe your battles look different, but are just as fierce. Either way, we all have stories and experiences that shape us. These experiences, whether triumphs or trials, form the bedrock of our personal wealth.

"If you don't come from a wealthy family, a wealthy family needs to come from you." This powerful quote resonates with many, but what if I told you that you're already wealthy beyond measure? I'm not talking about the kind of wealth that simply fills bank accounts. I'm referring to a more profound richness—one that money can't buy.

Let's redefine wealth. It's not just financial; it's the richness of your mind, the depth of your relationships, the abundance of your time, and yes, the potential of your finances. **Mental Wealth forms the foundation of personal branding, yet it's the #1 most overlooked aspect**—a critical mistake many make when crafting their professional image. Mental Wealth is the ability to laser-focus your attention and curate your thoughts, selecting only the most empowering ones to occupy your mind.

Now, grab whatever's handy – this book, a journal, your phone, even that coffee-stained napkin – because this is all about YOU. Together, we're shedding your liedentity and now we'll unveil the true extent of your mental wealth. Turn the page, and I'll show you how to "Promote Your D@mn Self" like a C.E.O. Because here's the truth: you are the C.E.O. of YOU. Write that down. Take a picture. Make it your screensaver. This is your moment to shine, to lead, to be the boss of your own story.

1. **Celebrate Your D@mn Achievements:**

Write down your top 5 accomplishments—and remember, they don't have to be work-related. Are you the first in your family to achieve something significant? Write it down. Did you accomplish something after being told you couldn't? That goes on the list too. Every win, every step forward, every moment you chose yourself—it all counts. This isn't about being humble or waiting for recognition. It's about boldly celebrating your wins so that others are inspired to reach for their dreams too.

Once you've compiled your list, read it aloud. Every. Single. Day. Make it your power mantra. Turn it into a song if that feels right. Do whatever it takes to internalize your achievements and feel the powerhouse that you truly are.

Remember, when you celebrate yourself, you're giving others permission to do the same. Your self-acknowledgment isn't just personal—it's revolutionary. It's building your mental wealth and inspiring others to do the same.

1. _____

2. _____

3. _____

4. _____

5. _____

2. Embrace Your Unique Story:

You think your journey is just a bunch of random stuff that happened? Nuh-uh. It's the secret sauce that makes you so irresistible in this bland world.

Every odd job you've had, every time you fell on your face and got back up, every crazy idea you turned into gold—that's not just your past, that's your power. Stop trying to fit into some boring box society's got laid out for you. The world's drowning in basic, and you're over here being a tall glass of "holy crap, who is that?!" Embrace it!

Your experiences? They're not just memories, they're money in the bank. That summer you spent waiting tables and learned how to handle even the nastiest customers with a smile? That's customer service gold. The time you backpacked across the country on a shoestring budget? That's resourcefulness that corporations would kill for.

When you share your real story, you're not just talking about yourself. You're giving permission to every other person out there who's afraid to be different. You're showing them that success doesn't look like one thing—it looks like you, in all your gorgeous, unique glory.

Write your unique story?

3. Own Continuous Self-Improvement:

I know you're carrying around a backpack full of "what-ifs" and "if-onlys." I see you replaying those moments where you think you messed up, where you didn't speak up, where you let someone else take credit for your hard work. That weight? It's exhausting, isn't it? It's holding you back from being the powerhouse you're meant to be. But here's the secret to lightening that load: forgiveness. It isn't just some airy-fairy concept—it's your ticket to freedom, your path to reclaiming your power.

When you forgive yourself for not being perfect, for making mistakes, for trusting the wrong people—you're not letting yourself off the hook. You're cutting the chains that have been holding you back. You're saying, "Yeah, that happened, but it doesn't define me." And when you do that? That's when you start to see yourself clearly. That's when you can finally use all that energy you've been wasting on regret and channel it into becoming unstoppable.

Now, let's turn this realization into action:

- Think about that big, scary goal you've been avoiding. The one that makes your heart race a little. Got it? Now, do one small thing towards it today. Right now. Send that email, make that call, write that first paragraph. Why? Because every time you take action, you're telling that voice of self-doubt to sit down and shut up.

Use this space to document your thoughts. Don't run from those scary thoughts. Capture them here on this page.

Remember, every act of forgiveness, every celebration of your achievements, every step towards your goals—it's all you reclaiming your power.

We've been talking about confidence, mental wealth, and authenticity. We've introduced you to the Authenticity over Approval method. But now it's time to lean in.

Promote Your D@mn Self isn't just some catchy title I slapped on this book. It's your personal revolution waiting to happen. You've got a unique voice, a perspective that can change lives, and value that this world desperately needs.

But if you're not promoting yourself, you're not just cheating yourself - you're robbing the world of your gifts.

Let me tell you something. The only person that's confused about your brilliance and potential is YOU.

You are a:

- Business **Now**
- Leader **Now**
- Keynote Speaker **Now**
- Author **Now**
- Coach **Now**
- Personal Brand **Now**
- Successful **Now**
- Living the life you dreamed of **NOW**!

Everything starts with a vision. What's yours?

Promoting yourself isn't just okay - it's your moral obligation. Why? Because you've got something unique to offer this world. Your experiences, your skills, your perspective - they're all part of a solution that someone out there is desperately seeking. When you hold back, you're not just shortchanging yourself, you're denying others the opportunity to benefit from what you know.

Think about it this way: If you had the cure for a disease, would you keep it to yourself? Of course not! You'd shout it from the rooftops. Well, your knowledge, your skills, your unique approach - that's your cure. It might be the cure for someone's business struggles, their career roadblocks, or even their personal challenges.

When you promote yourself effectively, you're not being arrogant or self-centered. You're being a beacon of hope. You're saying, "Hey, I've been where you are. I've faced those challenges. And I've found a way through. Let me show you how." That's not bragging - that's serving.

Consider this scenario: There's someone out there right now, lying awake at night, stressing over a problem that you know how to solve. They're losing sleep, losing money, maybe even losing hope. And you've got the answer they need. But if you're too scared to speak up, too modest to put yourself out there, what happens to that person? They keep struggling. They keep suffering. All because you were too afraid to say, "I can help."

Your silence isn't humility - it's selfishness. Your modesty isn't virtue - it's vanity. You're more concerned with how you might be perceived than with the good you could do. And your reluctance to shine? It's not just dimming your light - it's leaving others in the dark. So here's what I want you to do. Right now. Make a blood pact with yourself. Swear that you'll stop hiding in the shadows.

Promise that you'll start valuing yourself enough to shout your skills from the rooftops. Commit to promoting your knowledge like your life depends on it - because someone else's life or livelihood might actually depend on it.

The world is starving for what you've got. Your voice isn't just unique - it's necessary. In a sea of noise, your authentic voice could be the one that finally resonates with someone who's been searching for answers. Your ideas aren't just interesting - they're revolutionary. They have the power to change mindsets, transform businesses, and alter lives. Your expertise isn't just valuable - it's priceless. It's been forged in the fires of your own experiences, failures, and successes. It's a unique combination that no one else can replicate.

But all of that means nothing if you keep it locked up in your head. It's like having a fortune locked in a safe that you never open. It doesn't do anyone any good - not you, and certainly not the people who could benefit from your wealth of knowledge.

Promote Your D@mn Self is about creating a future where you're not just existing, but dominating. It's about stepping into your power and owning your expertise. It's about having the courage to say, "This is who I am, this is what I know, and this is how I can help." It's about altering the trajectory of your life - pushing past your comfort zone, embracing your potential, and achieving things you never thought possible.

But it doesn't stop there. When you promote yourself effectively, you're not just changing your own life. You're impacting the lives of hundreds, thousands, maybe even millions of others. Every person you reach with your message, every client you help, every audience you speak to - they all have the potential to take what they've learned from you and create a ripple effect of positive change in their own spheres of influence.

Fixing your mindset and growing your confidence will be revisited as we navigate through each part of the A.N.S.W.E.R. Method.
You are the A.N.S.W.E.R. to all of the questions, problems, concerns that you have. We will discuss in detail in the next few chapters how to apply the A.N.S.W.E.R. method to your life, career, and personal brand.

So, I'm asking you point-blank: Are you ready? Are you ready to step up, stand out, and make some serious impact? Are you prepared to create value so mind-blowing that everything else becomes irrelevant?

The next chapter is going to give you the blueprint of how to build a personal brand as an employee even if you have a boss that doesn't support your personal branding goals. We're going to dive into strategies in the coming chapters that'll make people's heads snap in your direction. You'll learn how to spark curiosity, command attention, and position yourself as the undisputed authority in your field. And we'll do it all while staying true to who you are at your core.

But first, you need to make that iron-clad commitment. Are you in? Are you ready to Promote Your D@mn Self like your life depends on it?

If the answer is YES, even if your voice trembles. I want to say

Welcome to the Movement

Turn the page when you're done playing small and ready to play big. Your empire awaits. It's time to embrace your brilliance, step into your power, and show the world what you're made of.

THINGS TO REMEMBER FROM THIS CHAPTER

Mental Wealth: The Confidence Secret They Don't Want You to Know

- That voice telling you you're not good enough? It's lying. Whether you're a shy introvert or a bold extrovert, you're sitting on a goldmine of untapped mental wealth. Society's been holding you back from cashing in. The power to grow your career, business, and personal brand starts with controlling what occupies your mental capacity.

Visualizing Confidence:

- Picture yourself six months from now, standing confidently in front of a mirror, your posture strong, and your eyes bright with determination. This future version of you has worked hard to build confidence, and it shows in every aspect of your life. You now Promote Your D@mn Self as a C.E.O. Your personal brand is strong, and people are starting to take notice.

Celebrate Your Achievements:

- Don't downplay your successes. Boldly acknowledge and celebrate them. This fosters self-confidence and inspires others.

Embrace Your Unique Story:

- Your journey is unique. Embrace and share your authentic story. This differentiates you from others and adds depth to your personal brand.

THINGS TO REMEMBER FROM THIS CHAPTER

Own Continuous Self-Improvement:

- Authenticity means embracing growth. Continuously seek self-improvement while staying true to your core identity and values. This journey is about celebrating your achievements, embracing your story, and committing to growth.

By prioritizing Authenticity over Approval, you can build a strong, genuine personal brand that stands out, fosters deeper connections, and brings greater career and business satisfaction.

YOUR NOTES:

Take a moment to reflect

YOUR NOTES:

Take a moment to reflect

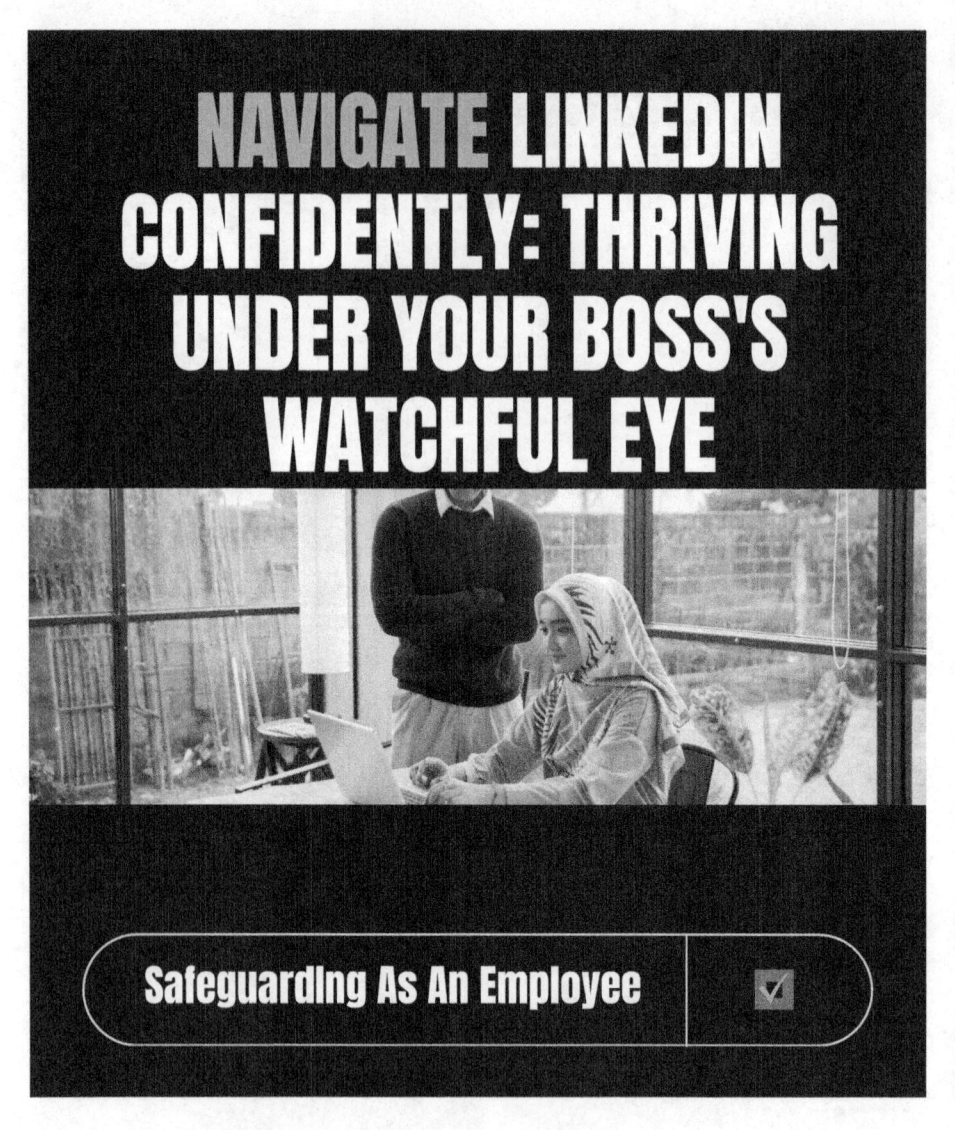

NAVIGATE LINKEDIN CONFIDENTLY: THRIVING UNDER YOUR BOSS'S WATCHFUL EYE

Safeguarding As An Employee ✓

What you will learn

Corporate loyalty meets personal ambition: The new playbook. Explore cutting-edge strategies to build your brand on LinkedIn, transforming perceived threats into win-win scenarios for you and your employer.

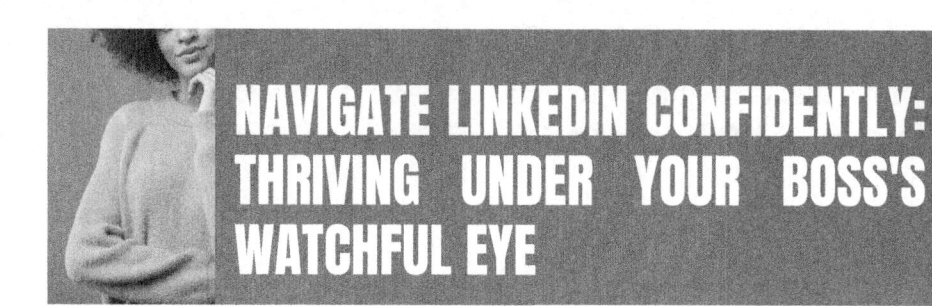

NAVIGATE LINKEDIN CONFIDENTLY: THRIVING UNDER YOUR BOSS'S WATCHFUL EYE

In the professional realm, there's an elephant in the room that we need to address: the paralyzing fear of engaging on LinkedIn under your boss's watchful eye. It's a peculiar paradox, isn't it? We barely flinch at the sight of beach body selfies or chandelier-swinging antics on Facebook, but LinkedIn? That's a whole different ballgame.

I've witnessed this hesitation firsthand throughout my two decades in the industry. You're excelling at work, yet when it comes to showcasing your talents on LinkedIn, it feels like you're teetering on the edge of a cliff. Trust me, I've been there, and I've guided countless professionals through this very dilemma.

Let me share a perspective that could revolutionize your approach to LinkedIn. Lean in close, because this insight might just be the catalyst you need to ignite your professional online

LINKEDIN ISN'T JUST ANOTHER SOCIAL MEDIA PLATFORM IT'S YOUR PROFESSIONAL SHOWCASE

presence. LinkedIn isn't merely another social media platform; it's your digital portfolio, a professional showcase. Your boss's presence on the platform shouldn't be a threat – but an opportunity to highlight your engagement and expertise in your field.

Let me share a story when I first realized this about LinkedIn. I'm sitting in my home office, probably sipping on my second kombucha of the day, when an email pings into my inbox. Lo and behold, it's an invitation to deliver a keynote speech on Personal Branding and Authenticity. My first thought? "WHATTTT, this is happening!" But here's the thing- I didn't seek out this opportunity. LinkedIn brought it to my virtual doorstep.

When I hopped on a call with the client, I was in for a surprise. They have done their homework, and I mean REALLY done it. They'd Googled me six ways to Sunday, poured over my LinkedIn reviews like they were studying for a final exam, and binged on podcasts I'd been featured on like it was the latest Netflix series. They'd even done a deep dive into my LinkedIn content.

It hit me like a ton of bricks - they knew more about my professional journey than some of my closest colleagues. Talk about a power shift in negotiations! I felt like I was holding all the aces, and let me tell you, it felt damn good.

This whole experience was a massive wake-up call. It hammered home the sheer power of social media in ways I'd never fully appreciated before. My personal brand and the content I'd been consistently putting out there? That was the real MVP. It closed the deal before I even opened my mouth.

So, let me lay it out for you straight: A powerful personal brand isn't just nice to have - it can be the make-or-break factor in landing your next big opportunity. It's your secret weapon, your golden ticket, your 'I-am-the-best-choice' card.

This isn't about bragging; it's about illuminating the immense potential at your fingertips. You can absolutely learn new skill and take a course on LinkedIn that can get you promoted. You can land clients that make your bank account do a happy dance. You can position yourself as the go-to expert in your field. All through LinkedIn. It's time to stop playing small and start showing up on

LinkedIn like the C.E.O. of your life and career. Your future self will thank you for it.

So, what are you waiting for? What are you afraid of? Probably the same thing that I was afraid of and the thing that many of my clients are afraid of.

I'm about to share a truth that most personal branding experts keep under wraps. Despite having cultivated a stellar corporate reputation and amassing a track record that would turn heads in any professional circle, I was terrified of putting myself out there on LinkedIn. Yes, you read that correctly.

The thoughts that kept me up at night were all too familiar: "What if my boss thinks I'm job hunting? What if I lose their trust? What if I get fired?" Trust me, I get it. Trust is a big deal, and so is job security. The thought of your boss stumbling across your posts and somehow using it against you – it's a legitimate concern that paralyzes many professionals.

I am going to give you some strategies but acknowledging this fear is the first step towards conquering it. And the truth? If you're doing it right, your LinkedIn presence should actually impress your boss, not scare them.

My journey from LinkedIn-phobic to LinkedIn-empowered wasn't an overnight transformation. It was a gradual process of realizing that my expertise and experiences were valuable not just within the confines of my office, but to a broader professional community. And that realization? It was liberating.

So, if you're feeling that knot in your stomach at the thought of ramping up your LinkedIn presence, know that you're not alone.

Even those of us with enviable careers have stood where you stand. The key is to recognize that your voice matters, your insights are valuable, and your professional journey could be the inspiration someone else needs.

Now, you've probably heard those LinkedIn influencers preaching that your personal brand is yours alone, and you don't need anyone's permission to strut your stuff online. Well, let me burst that bubble - it's not entirely true, especially if you're on someone else's payroll.

Here's a reality check for you: According to CareerBuilder, nearly half of employers are playing Big Brother with their employees' social media. Many companies have strict social media policies that dictate what you can and cannot post, even on your personal accounts. So before you hit that 'share' button on that spicy political meme or that scathing review of your company's latest product, think twice. There is a 50-50 chance that your boss is scrolling through your social media and LinkedIn profile right now judging your weekend shenanigans. And it's not just about catching you in compromising situations. Feeling paranoid yet? But why would your boss be creeping on your LinkedIn? Let me count the ways:

- They might've stumbled upon your profile while LinkedIn surfing.
- They could be sizing you up for a promotion or transfer.
- Someone might've tipped them off about something funky on your profile.
- They might be making sure you're not tarnishing the company's reputation.
- If they suspect you're planning to jump ship, they might be checking for any dirty laundry you're airing online.

So, what's a savvy professional to do? Here's my game plan:

- Know your company's social media policy like the back of your hand.
- If you're on good terms with your boss, have an honest chat about your LinkedIn goals. Loop in HR too. Get it all in writing - CYA, my friend.

When I decided to build my personal brand, I took a bold step that might seem counterintuitive at first: I laid all my cards on the table.

I approached my management team and HR, openly discussing my side hustles, my LinkedIn aspirations, and my vision for professional growth. It was a nerve-wracking conversation, to be sure. But the outcome? It was nothing short of transformative.
To my surprise and delight, not only did they support my endeavors, but they actively embraced them. My team began engaging with my content, amplifying my voice beyond what I could have achieved alone. But it didn't stop there. They saw the value in what I was doing and created opportunities for me to share my knowledge with our global workforce of over 30,000 employees. Talk about a win-win situation!

I understand your concerns. The thought of your boss scrutinizing your LinkedIn activity can be daunting. But let me assure you, with the right approach, you can turn this perceived challenge into a remarkable opportunity.

Here's how we can break it down:
- Transparency is key. Be open about your professional goals and online presence.
- Align your personal brand with company values. Show how your growth benefits the organization.

- Engage your superiors. Invite them to be part of your journey.
- Demonstrate value. Use your platform to highlight your achievements with the company and industry insights.

Remember, a strong personal brand doesn't threaten your current position – it enhances it. Trust me, with the right approach, you can turn this into a win-win situation. Let's break it down:

Template : Talking To Your Manager And HR

Hey [Manager's Name],

I wanted to discuss something with you. I've been thinking about ways to grow professionally and contribute more to our team. I'm planning to become more active on LinkedIn to build my personal brand. I believe this could benefit both me and [Company Name]. Can we chat about how I can do this in a way that aligns with our company's goals?

Best,
[NAME]

Talking Points:

- Emphasize how your personal brand can positively reflect on the company
- Discuss sharing company content and achievements (in accordance with company policies)
- Highlight networking opportunities that could lead to potential clients or partnerships
- Mention how your growth can bring new skills and insights to your role

Template : If Your Boss Isn't Supportive

Hi [Manager's Name],

I understand your concerns, [Manager's Name]. My intention isn't to look for a new job or compete with the company. Instead, I see this as an opportunity to grow professionally and bring more value to our team. How about we set some guidelines together to ensure my LinkedIn activity aligns with [Company Name]'s interests?

Best,
(NAME)

What to Do:

- Listen to their concerns and address them specifically
- Suggest a trial period with regular check-ins
- Offer to share your content plans in advance
- Propose focusing on industry insights rather than company-specific information
- Highlight successful examples of employees at other companies who've built personal brands

Remember, it's about framing this as a benefit for everyone. You're not trying to outshine the company – you're aiming to be a star player on the team.

If you're still met with resistance, you might need to tone down your LinkedIn activity during work hours and focus more on general industry insights rather than company-specific content. But don't give up on your personal brand journey.

Now, I know not everyone's going to have it this good. I hear you —what if your boss isn't the supportive type? What if they see your growing influence as a threat? Well, my friend, that's when you need to get strategic. Remember, your personal brand isn't just about your current job; it's about your entire career trajectory. If your boss can't appreciate your growth, it might be a sign that you've outgrown your current role anyway.

So if you can't get buy-in from the higher-ups, here's plan B:

Build your brand quietly until you're ready to make some noise. Lock down your LinkedIn privacy settings. If you're job hunting, be smart about it. Share content that makes you look good in your current role while catching the eye of recruiters.

Leverage your expertise subtly by engaging in industry conversations. Comment thoughtfully on posts from thought leaders and peers, offering insights that showcase your knowledge without explicitly promoting yourself. This approach allows you to build credibility and connections organically, flying under your company's radar while still making an impact in your professional community.

Create content that serves a dual purpose. Craft posts and articles that highlight your team's successes or your company's innovations, positioning yourself as a dedicated employee while simultaneously demonstrating your individual talents. This strategy not only safeguards your current position but also paints you as a valuable asset to potential future employers who appreciate team players with initiative.

Cultivate a personal passion project that complements your

professional skills. Whether it's a podcast, a blog, or volunteer work in your field, pursue something that allows you to flex your expertise outside of work hours. This gives you a safe space to build your brand without directly competing with your day job. Plus, it provides a ready-made talking point for networking conversations, allowing you to discuss your abilities and ambitions without explicitly job hunting.

Remember, building a personal brand while employed is like walking a tightrope. But with the right strategy, you can create a powerful online presence without burning bridges or risking your job.

> **NOW, LET'S TALK ABOUT THAT CODE-SWITCHING FEAR. YOU'RE WORRIED ABOUT BEING "PROFESSIONAL" VERSUS BEING "YOURSELF," RIGHT?**

If you're not familiar with the term, code switching, let me break it down for you. Code switching at work is like having a split personality, but on purpose.

You know how you talk to your friends when you're chilling, right? All casual, maybe throwing in some slang, not focusing on having perfect grammar. But then you step into the office, and suddenly you're all "Indeed, I concur with your astute observation, colleague."

That's code switching. It's when you change up your language, tone, and even body language depending on who you're talking to or where you are. At work, it usually means putting on your "professional" voice - sounding more formal, using bigger words, maybe even changing your accent a bit.

It's like having different masks for different situations. With the boss, you're all prim and proper. With your work friends, you might loosen up a bit. Then you're on the phone with a client, and bam - you're back to being Mr. or Ms. "Professional".

Some people do it without even thinking, while others find it exhausting. It can be a survival tactic, especially for people from marginalized groups who feel they need to "fit in" with the dominant culture at work.

Honestly, it's unsettling for someone to feel the pressure to change who they are just to be taken seriously. But unfortunately, that's the reality for some people.

I was at a personal branding workshop in Atlanta, trying not to sweat my butt off in the summer heat. In walks this woman who's been grinding it out at a stuffy insurance company for years. She's decked out like she's heading to a corporate funeral - black blazer, black skirt, red top, pumps, stud earrings, and a blunt-cut black bob that screams "I mean business." Oh, and let's not forget the red lips - because God forbid we forget we're women, right?

Meanwhile, there I am, cool as a can be in my pastel blue two-piece short set, rocking big hoop earrings and cognac sandals. Why? Because it's on-brand for me, I look cute, and I refuse to melt in the Atlanta heat for anyone's corporate expectations.

We get to talking, and this woman drops a truth bomb that hits me right in the gut. She's mastered the art of code-switching like it's an Olympic sport. Why? Because she's often the only woman or the only Black woman in the room. She's dreaming of rocking some color in her hair but is terrified of being judged as she climbs the corporate ladder.

I asked her if her company encourages that whole "bring your authentic self to work" culture. She says yes, but then drops the real truth - that doesn't mean she actually can. And damn, if that doesn't sum up the whole problem in a nutshell. Have you been there? Are you still there?

It got me thinking - how many of us are standing in our own way like this? How many of us are our own worst enemies when it comes to embracing our authenticity?

I encouraged her to take baby steps towards embracing her true self as a leader. But let's be real - it's not just about individual choices. This is a systemic issue that hits women and people of color particularly hard.

We're often so afraid to challenge the status quo or truly embrace our authenticity that we end up dimming our own light. We contort ourselves into these corporate-approved versions of professionalism that have nothing to do with our actual skills or leadership abilities.

So here's my challenge to you: Take a hard look at how you're showing up at work. Are you being true to yourself, or are you wearing a corporate costume? Are you letting fear dictate your choices?

Remember, your authenticity is your superpower. It's what makes you unique, memorable, and frankly, irreplaceable. Don't let outdated notions of "professionalism" rob you of your magic. It's time to start pushing those boundaries, friends.

Have fun with your hair. Wear those bold earrings. Wear sneakers with your suit. Let your personality shine through in your work. Because at the end of the day, a workplace that can't handle the authentic you doesn't deserve your talent.

So go ahead, be unapologetically you. The corporate world needs more of that, not less. And who knows? You might just inspire others to do the same. Let's start an authenticity revolution, one bold choice at a time! And here's a little secret: the most powerful personal brands are authentic. People can smell fakeness from a mile away. The trick is to find the sweet spot between your professional expertise and your genuine personality.

So, you are probably thinking, how do we start building this brand without setting off alarm bells? Regardless of where you are in your authenticity and/or professional journey, I want to give you some tips on how to get started. Let's break it down into some actionable steps:

1. **Start Slow and Steady:** Don't go from zero to a hundred overnight. Begin by updating your profile, making sure it reflects your current role and achievements. This is something any good employee would do, so it won't raise eyebrows.

2. **Engage Before You Create:** Before you start posting, spend time liking and commenting on others' posts. Focus on industry news, thought leadership pieces, and updates from your company. This shows you're engaged in your field without putting yourself in the spotlight just yet.

3. **Share Company Content:** When you do start posting, begin by sharing updates from your company's LinkedIn page. Add a brief, positive comment. This demonstrates you're a team player and

proud of your workplace.

4. **Gradual Personal Content:** Slowly introduce your own thoughts. Start with simple things like sharing an article you found interesting, with a brief comment on why. As you get more comfortable, you can share insights from conferences or industry events you attend.

5. **Find Your Voice:** Remember that authenticity we talked about? Use it here. If you're naturally funny, let some humor shine through (professionally, of course). If you're passionate about certain aspects of your work, let that enthusiasm come across.

6. **Consistency is Key:** Set a realistic schedule for yourself. Maybe it's one post a week to start. Consistency builds your presence more effectively than sporadic bursts of activity.

7. **Network Strategically:** Connect with colleagues, industry peers, and thought leaders. Engaging with their content can often be less daunting than creating your own, and it still builds your presence.

> **NOW, LET'S REVISIT THAT NAGGING FEAR ABOUT PUTTING YOUR JOB AT RISK.**

Unless you're sharing confidential information or badmouthing your company (which I know you wouldn't do), you're not risking your job. Building a personal brand while employed is not without its challenges. One of the primary concerns is the potential conflict of interest with your current employer. There's a delicate balance to strike between promoting your individual expertise and maintaining loyalty to your company. Additionally, the time commitment required to cultivate a personal brand can be substantial, potentially impacting your work performance if not managed carefully.

And sometimes it's the story that we tell ourselves and not necessarily the fact that we are putting our jobs at risk. I am not saying that putting your job at risk can't happen but we as humans often go to the extreme. The mind is a tricky chick.

Despite these challenges, the value of a well-executed personal brand in your career can be immense. It can position you as a thought leader in your industry, attracting networking opportunities and potential job offers/promotions. A strong personal brand can also increase your perceived value within your current organization, potentially leading to promotions or more rewarding projects.

Let me tell you about Pam. OMG! Pam's story... it's like a rose growing out of concrete. She was the first in her family to go to college, earned a master's degree, and pulled herself out of poverty. Now she's this respected director at an organization that's all about civic leadership, community investment, and philanthropy. Sounds impressive, right? But here's the thing- Pam thought LinkedIn was pretentious. Can you believe it? Psssttt, I can because I thought the exact same thing.

Pam's got dreams, big ones. She wants to write a book, work with girls' groups, tackle generational poverty head-on, and have those tough conversations that actually change systems. She's all about women's ministry, being a free bird, and making a collective impact. But there was this disconnect. All these amazing ideas, all this wisdom, and she was keeping it locked up inside.

One day, we're in one of our coaching sessions, and I'm listening to Pam talk about her fears. She's worried about how to live with integrity as a Christian, how to balance passion and just being. And then it hit me - Pam was so focused on her own feelings that she was forgetting about the people she could serve.

That's when I dropped the truth bomb: "Pam, it's time to Promote Your Damn Self."

I saw her eyes widen, and I knew I had to explain. "Listen," I said, "showing up on LinkedIn isn't about you. It's about meeting the person who needs you right where they are. It's about pushing your mission forward even when no one's clapping, liking, or commenting. It's about getting out of your head and into your purpose."

And you know what? Something shifted in Pam that day. She realized that by holding back, she wasn't just shortchanging herself - she was depriving others of her gifts. She started to see herself as a "social cardiologist," someone who could change hearts and minds, bending them towards justice.

Now, Pam's out there on LinkedIn, sharing her truth, and championing the fight against intergenerational poverty. She's not just posting - she's truth-telling. And let me tell you, that's what's changing hearts.

So, my friend, if you're sitting there feeling like Pam used to, worried about what people might think or say, remember this: your voice matters. Your experiences, your wisdom - someone out there needs to hear it. Don't let fear keep you silent. It's time to step up, shine your light, and yes, Promote Your D@mn Self. Because when you do, you're not just changing your life - you're changing the world. Remember, your personal brand is an investment in yourself. It's about playing the long game. Every post, every connection, every insight you share is a deposit in your professional future. It might feel uncomfortable at first, but that's where growth happens.

Here are some immediate actions you can take to boost your confidence and start growing your influence and personal brand:

- **Create an internal newsletter:** Offer to start a company-wide or department-specific newsletter highlighting industry trends, best practices, and employee achievements. This positions you as an in-house thought leader and information curator.
- **Propose a lunch-and-learn series:** Organize informal learning sessions where employees share skills or insights. By leading some sessions and facilitating others, you demonstrate leadership and a commitment to continuous learning.
- **Develop a personal project aligned with company goals:** Initiate a side project that benefits your company or industry. This could be anything from creating a productivity tool to writing a white paper on an emerging trend.
- **Volunteer as a company representative:** Offer to represent your company at industry events, career fairs, or community outreach programs. This expands your network while showcasing your commitment to your employer.
- **Start an internal mentorship program:** Propose and coordinate a mentorship initiative within your company, connecting junior and senior employees. This demonstrates leadership and a dedication to fostering talent.

For employees with unsupportive managers, consider these alternatives:

- **Focus on industry presence:** Build your brand within your industry rather than your specific company. Contribute to industry publications, participate in online forums, or start a

professional blog without mentioning your employer.
- **Leverage professional associations:** Many industries have professional associations that offer opportunities for leadership roles, speaking engagements, or committee work. These can bolster your personal brand without directly involving your employer.
- **Skill-based volunteering:** Offer your professional skills to non-profit organizations. This allows you to expand your network and showcase your expertise in a context separate from your day job.
- **Create educational content:** Start a YouTube channel, blog, podcast, or write an eBook about your area of expertise. Focus on general industry knowledge rather than company-specific information.
- **Cultivate a personal advisory board:** Build relationships with mentors and industry peers outside your company. They can provide guidance, opportunities, and act as references without involving your current employer.

Remember, the key is to focus on adding value to your industry and developing your skills in ways that don't directly conflict with your work responsibilities.

YOUR WEEKLY THOUGHT EXCERCISE

On LinkedIn consider, writing one post a week, even if you don't publish it right away. This helps you find your voice and build a content backlog.

Why this works: Writing is thinking made visible.

By committing to writing one post a week, you're giving yourself permission to explore your thoughts and ideas in a structured way. This isn't about perfection – it's about practice. Even if you don't hit 'publish' right away, you're building a valuable skill: the ability to articulate your professional thoughts clearly and concisely. Plus, you're creating a content bank for yourself. On days when inspiration is running low, you'll have a stash of ideas to pull from.

Pro tip: Set a timer for 20 minutes and just write. Don't edit as you go – just get your thoughts down. You can polish it later. Topics can range from lessons learned on a recent project to your take on industry news or even a book review related to your field.

Expand Your Horizons, One Connection at a Time

Aim to connect with one new person each week—whether it's someone you respect in your industry or a colleague you haven't had the chance to engage with. True connections are what create a robust network.

Why it matters: Your network truly is a reflection of your value. But it's not about amassing contacts; it's about fostering authentic, mutually beneficial relationships.

By reaching out to one new person each week, you're gradually expanding your professional circle. This isn't just good for job hunting – it's how you stay on top of industry trends, get exposed to new ideas, and sometimes even find mentors or mentees.

Pro tip: When you reach out, make it personal. Use the template provided on page #21. Mention why you're interested in connecting – maybe you enjoyed their recent post, or you share a mutual connection. Offer something of value, even if it's just an interesting article you think they might enjoy.

Stay in the Know

Set up Google Alerts for topics in your industry. This gives you a steady stream of content to potentially share and comment on.

Why this works: Knowledge is power, my friend. By setting up alerts, you're essentially creating your own personal news feed of industry-relevant information. This serves multiple purposes:

- It keeps you informed about the latest trends and developments in your field.

- It provides you with a constant stream of potential content to share or comment on.

- It gives you talking points for networking events or job interviews.

- It helps you spot opportunities or challenges in your industry before others do.

Pro tip: Don't just share these alerts verbatim. Add your own thoughts or questions when you post them. This shows that you're not just passing along information, but actively engaging with and thinking about industry news.

Bonus

Promote Your D@mn Self: The Time-Crunched Creator's Secret Weapon

Pro tip: We've all been there - a brilliant idea strikes, but time is slipping through your fingers like sand. You know you should post something, but crafting the perfect content feels daunting. This is where the magic of AI comes in, my friend. As someone juggling the tightrope walk of being both an employee and an entrepreneur, I've learned that efficiency isn't just nice - it's necessary. And let me tell you, AI has been a game-changer in my content creation process.

AI is like having a super-smart friend who's read basically everything on the internet. That's kind of what AI is like. It's a computer program that can understand and chat with you almost like a person.

Not all AI tools are created equal. Sure, ChatGPT gets all the hype, but for us content creators, there's a secret weapon that's been flying under the radar: Claude AI.

Why Claude? It's like having a brainstorming friend, a research assistant, and a wordsmith all rolled into one. It doesn't just spit out generic content; it helps you refine your ideas, offers different perspectives, and can even adapt to your unique voice and style. (I used Claude AI as a thought partner while writing this book). Give it a try, you can't break it.

Here's how to make the most of AI tools for content creation:

- Feed it your half-baked idea. The more context and information you give, the better.
- Ask it to expand on the concept or provide different angles.
- Use its output as a springboard for your own creativity.
- Refine and personalize the content to make it authentically you.

Remember, AI is a tool, not a replacement for your unique insights and experiences. Use it to to spark new ideas, or to help structure your thoughts when you're pressed for time.

So the next time you're feeling the pressure to post but coming up short on time or inspiration, give Claude AI a try. It might just be the competitive advantage that keeps your content flowing, even on your busiest days.

Now, here's the confidence boost you need: By taking these actions, you're not just building a personal brand – you're investing in yourself. You're saying to the world (and more importantly, to yourself) that your thoughts and experiences have value. That you're committed to growth and learning. That you're not content to just clock in and clock out, but that you're an engaged, thoughtful professional who's actively shaping your career.

Remember, confidence isn't about knowing everything. It's about being comfortable with what you know and being curious about what you don't. Every time you engage on LinkedIn, whether it's liking a post, commenting in a group, or sharing your own thoughts, you're flexing your professional muscles. And just like in the gym, every rep makes you stronger.

You've got unique experiences, insights, and perspectives. The world needs to hear them. So take these steps, start small, and watch as your confidence grows along with your influence. You're not just building a personal brand – you're shaping the professional you want to be. And let me tell you, that professional is someone to be reckoned with.

Listen, I know it feels daunting. That little voice in your head questioning every move? I've been there. But here's what I want you to remember: You are not just your job title. You're a professional with unique experiences, insights, and value to offer. Your personal brand is about showcasing that value to the world.

You've got this. And you know what? I'm excited for you. Because once you push past that fear and start putting yourself out there, amazing things happen. Opportunities find you. Your confidence grows. And before you know it, you're not just building a personal brand – you're building the career you've always wanted.

So, take a deep breath. Start small. Be consistent. And remember, I'm in your corner. Your future self is going to thank you for taking this step. Now, let's go make some LinkedIn magic happen!

Important Note:

LinkedIn is widely regarded as one of the safest social media platforms, and for your own protection, I strongly advise against the following actions:

- Creating a second LinkedIn profile. LinkedIn is the safest social media platform and also advises against this.

- If you have concerns about your employer monitoring your activity, it's recommended to maintain your current profile. Instead, consider unfollowing and removing connections associated with your current employer, and utilize the privacy settings to block their access.

Despite potential suggestions from other sources, adhering to these practices ensures that you build your brand with integrity from the outset, safeguarding your professional reputation and privacy.

Once you've had a conversation with your boss and HR, assuming that it went well, talk about it on LinkedIn. Create a post and tell your connections about the conversation at a high level, share what you learned, and what you are excited about. Take the opportunity to teach your connections what you will be doing moving forward and tell them how they can help you. People love to help. When you create this post, let me help you. Tag me so that I can engage with you and your connections in the comments.

Use the hashtag:

#ShantelTaughtME!

TAKE IT FROM SHANTEL ...

It's crucial to maintain a visible and engaged presence on LinkedIn. By doing so thoughtfully and strategically, your next job, speaking engagement, client, and opportunity will come to you organically, eliminating the need for active outreach.

TRUTH MOMENT

Regardless of whether your boss is supportive or not, your well-being and security should always be a top priority. It's crucial to maintain visibility on LinkedIn to enjoy its benefits without risking your livelihood. My aim is to see you thrive, not face unnecessary hardship.

Utilize the power of LinkedIn groups to cultivate supportive communities and create safe spaces for job searching, building your business, or growing your connections. When engaging in discussions, consider taking conversations to direct messages (DMs) or platforms outside of LinkedIn where you have more control and less concern about corporate surveillance. Your success and peace of mind matter, and I'm here to help you protect both.

THINGS TO REMEMBER FROM THIS CHAPTER

Have the tough conversation with HR and your boss:

Discuss your LinkedIn goals. Transparency about your intentions can build trust and avoid misunderstandings. Discuss how your LinkedIn activity aligns with company goals and your professional development. Get their support in writing if possible, to protect yourself and clarify expectations. Remember, you're not alone in your fears about this conversation - many professionals face the same challenge. If your company is unreceptive, consider if this aligns with your long-term career aspirations.

Your LinkedIn presence can be an asset, not a liability:

This is especially true when your LinkedIn presence is managed strategically. A well-crafted LinkedIn profile showcases your professional growth and engagement in your field. Your activity can impress your current employer and attract new opportunities simultaneously.

Being visible on LinkedIn doesn't mean you're job hunting:

Your visibility on LinkedIn actually shows engagement in your field. Active participation demonstrates your commitment to professional development. Sharing industry insights and engaging in discussions positions you as a thought leader.

THINGS TO REMEMBER FROM THIS CHAPTER

Use privacy settings and group discussions:

Use these spaces to your advantage if you have concerns about employer monitoring. Adjust your settings to control who sees your activity. Participate in LinkedIn groups for more focused, potentially private discussions.

Balance professionalism with your genuine personality:

By doing so you can create a memorable online presence. Find the sweet spot between corporate expectations and your authentic self. Let your unique perspective and experiences inform your content and interactions.

> **LET'S TAKE ACTION:**

Start your "15-Minute LinkedIn Ritual" today. Set aside 15 minutes to scroll through your feed, like and comment thoughtfully on at least three posts. This simple habit will help you build confidence, engage with your network, and gradually increase your visibility on the platform.

Your unique experiences and insights have value. By taking small, consistent steps to build your presence, you're investing in your professional future. Remember, your personal brand is about more than your current job – it's about the professional you aspire to be.

YOUR NOTES:

Take a moment to reflect

YOUR NOTES:

*T*ake a moment to reflect

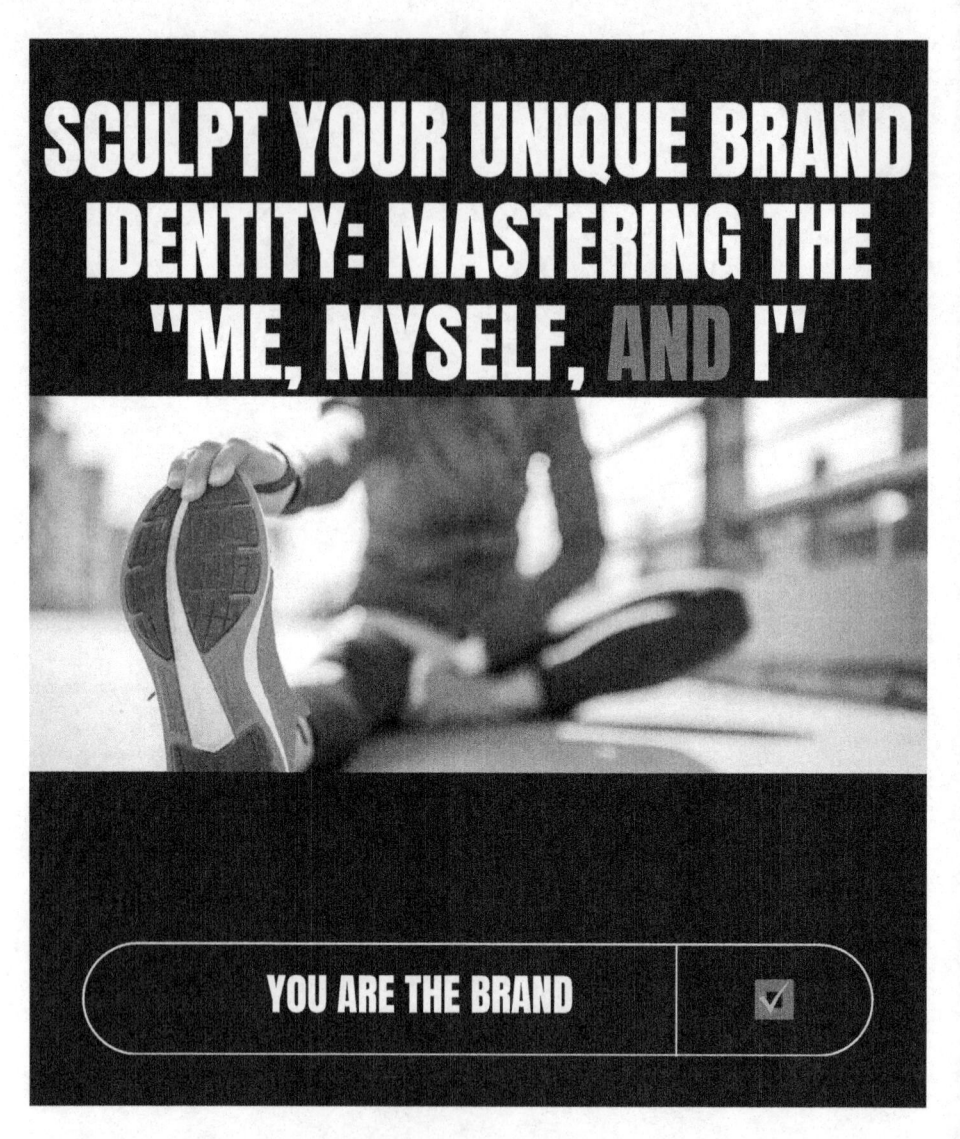

SCULPT YOUR UNIQUE BRAND IDENTITY: MASTERING THE "ME, MYSELF, AND I"

YOU ARE THE BRAND ☑

What you will learn

Craft a LinkedIn profile that turns heads and opens doors. Learn how to distill your professional essence into a compelling digital narrative that makes decision-makers take notice.

SCULPT YOUR UNIQUE BRAND IDENTITY: MASTERING THE "ME, MYSELF, AND I"

So there I was, at this massive conference, nominated for leader of the year (no big deal, right?). I'm sitting at a table when this lady taps me on the shoulder and goes, "Are you Shantel Love from LinkedIn?" Now, me being me, I couldn't resist a little joke: "Depends—do I owe you money?" We had a good laugh, but then things got real.

This exec tells me she's been following my LinkedIn posts, liking how I big up my team and my brand. But personally she's struggling to do the same for herself. When I asked why, her answer hit me like a ton of bricks.

She said pushing her team's awesomeness came easy because she believed in them. But when it came to tooting her own horn? Cue the self-doubt parade. She was worried about coming off as bragging or self-obsessed.

Sound familiar? I bet you've been there too, right? Downplaying your wins, hesitating to show off your skills on LinkedIn. It's like we're all scared of being "that person" who can't shut up about how great they are.

Self-promotion isn't arrogance—it's authenticity and owning your value. LinkedIn is your platform to showcase your expertise, share insights, and let the world see your worth.

Think about that exec I met. She had the goods but couldn't sell them. Your LinkedIn journey? It's about crushing those fears and finding your voice. It's about building that confidence in yourself and your skills, 'cause damn it, you deserve the spotlight!

I once sat on a panel with this LinkedIn exec who dropped some serious gems. She said your LinkedIn brand is like having your own Super Bowl ad. Let that sink in for a sec. The Super Bowl—millions of eyeballs glued to the screen, soaking up every story and message. LinkedIn is your playground, my friend.

It's not about being a showoff. It's about standing tall and proud, sharing your magic with the world. It's about making sure your voice cuts through all the noise out there.

Let's also take a lesson from Snoop Dogg, American rapper, record producer, and actor, who once famously said upon winning an award, "I want to thank me for believing in me, I want to thank me for doing all this hard work." It's a reminder that celebrating your achievements and acknowledging your hard work isn't arrogance—it's recognizing the truth and giving credit where it's due.

As you navigate your LinkedIn journey, remember that building a personal brand takes time and consistency. Embrace opportunities to showcase your achievements, share your insights, and connect with others in meaningful ways. Each interaction and post is a chance to strengthen your brand and expand your influence.

If you're like many of my mentees, you might be following me to this point in the book and you may even be feeling inspired, yet still have questions like "How do I start building my personal brand?" Don't worry, I've got you covered.

You've probably heard about personal branding and thought, "Isn't that just for entrepreneurs and influencers?" Well, guess what? It's not. Personal branding is just as important if you're working a 9 to 5. Think of it as your professional fingerprint, something uniquely you that sets you apart in your industry.

Take a moment: Google your name and see what comes up. This is your digital footprint. Is it representing you the way you want?

Personal branding serves as your distinctive signature in the professional realm—it's the way you present yourself, highlighting your skills, strengths, and unique qualities. The essential piece here is not to assume that others are aware of your value, skills, and strengths. Think of it as the narrative you share about yourself, crafted to connect with your audience. It's not merely about what you do, but how you do it and why it is significant.

Think of it this way: It's like curating your own brand identity, just like your favorite influencers or companies do. It's about being intentional with how you want to be perceived—whether you're aiming for recognition in your field, attracting new opportunities, or simply building credibility among your peers.

I know the concept of personal branding might seem like corporate jargon, but let me take you back to a career-defining moment that made me a true believer - a moment when my personal brand wasn't just a nice-to-have, it was my lifeline.

After years of grinding, I finally landed my dream director position. Leading a team of team of highly intelligent sales consultant, and I was the outsider "business woman". A 35% pay bump in my pocket, I felt really good.

Then, reality decided to throw me a curveball.

Just days into my new role, I sensed a disturbance in the force. Enter "Jane Doe" - a team member who'd been with the company since I was in diapers. She hadn't applied for my position, but boy, did she think it was her birthright.

As I'm chatting with an executive in the hallway, Jane joins the conversation uninvited. With a smile that didn't match her eye, she starts "sharing her thoughts" about my work. And then, she drops a bombshell that nearly stopped my heart:

"You know," she says to the executive, "I think I should mentor Shantel for a year to help her get acclimated to the role. After all, I have more experience."

My first thought? "Wow, the audacity!" But then, I took a deep breath and checked in with myself. I triggered what I like to call my "professional composure button."

Time froze. My blood boiled then turned to ice. At that moment, I realized my career could be a risk.

My first instinct? Panic. But then, something kicked in - something that would change the course of my career forever... Silence.

The silence felt endless. But then, the division executive spoke up.

"We picked the right person," he said firmly. "Shantel is the right person, and there's no need for mentorship. She will lead this team to success, as she has done year after year. We made the right choice, and I stand behind that decision."

In that moment, I realized something profound. My personal brand – the reputation I had built over years of consistent performance, the relationships I had nurtured, the value I had consistently delivered – had spoken for me when I couldn't speak for myself.

I discovered that what I had been doing along was called of Cognitive Dissonance Branding. Cognitive Dissonance Branding is the strategic incorporation of seemingly contradictory elements into your personal brand to create a more memorable, authentic, and compelling professional identity. This approach played a big role when a colleague tried to sabotage my career in front of the executive leader of the division. Cognitive Dissonance Branding is where your seeming contradictions become your greatest strength. My colleague Jane, thought she'd expose my weaknesses. Instead, she unknowingly highlighted the unique blend of skills and experiences that made me invaluable.

I wasn't just a sales director. I was also a creative problem-solver with a gift for storytelling. This unexpected combination allowed me to present complex information in compelling ways, a skill my manager and executive leaders had come to rely on.

My personal brand spoke louder than any attempted sabotage. Here's what I learned:
- Authenticity over Acceptance: Don't hide parts of yourself to fit a mold.
- Embrace your quirks: Your unusual combination of skills is your superpower.
- Show, don't tell: Let your work demonstrate your unique value.

START WITH TAKING THIS PERSONAL BRANDING ASSESSMENT:

So, how do you actually create a personal brand?

Step 1: Self-Reflection

It's so important to really get to know yourself and what you want to be known for. Take a moment to think about your strengths, the values that matter most to you, and what you're truly passionate about. Consider your unique experiences and how they've influenced the way you see the world. This kind of self-reflection can be incredibly powerful and guide you toward a fulfilling path.

Step 2: Define Your Core Values:

Defining your core values is like getting to the heart of what really matters to you. Think about it like this: what principles do you hold so dear that they guide your decisions and actions, even when things get tough?

Start by reflecting on moments in your life when you felt genuinely happy and fulfilled. What was happening then? Who were you with? What were you doing? These moments often align with your core values.

Also, consider the times when you felt deeply uncomfortable or frustrated. What was it about those situations that clashed with your beliefs or principles? This can help you identify what you want to avoid and what you stand for.

Write down a list of values that resonate with you. It might include things like honesty, kindness, growth, adventure, or family. Then, narrow it down to the top few that feel most essential to who you are.

What values do you hold most dear in your professional life?

_____
_____
_____
_____

Crafting Your Personal Brand Statement

So we're at the part where we're crafting your personal brand statement. This is where things get really exciting because we're about to sum up all that awesome stuff about you in one sentence.

1. Personal Brand Statement Formula:

[Your Name] is a [Your Profession] who helps [Target Audience] achieve [Benefit] through [Unique Approach].

Example:
Jemisha Jones is a digital marketing specialist who helps small businesses increase their online presence through data-driven strategies and creative content.

2. Write Your Personal Brand Statement:

_____
_____
_____

Keep this personal brand statement handy and use it in your LinkedIn headline.

Use the formula above but tweak it about. Use I (Action Verb) statements. Action verbs are words like: create, build, empower, support, assist, etc,.

Example: I empower small businesses to exceed sales goals and crush quotas by mastering the art of subtle selling.

Audit Your Current Online Presence:

Auditing your current online presence means taking a close, detailed look at how you and your brand are represented across the internet. It's about understanding what your digital footprint looks like and making sure it aligns with the image you want to project.

Check Social Media Profiles: Review all your social media accounts—Facebook, Twitter, LinkedIn, Instagram, etc. Make sure your profiles are up-to-date, professional, and reflect your personal brand. Look at your profile pictures, bios, and the content you've shared.

List your current social media profiles and professional networking sites (e.g., LinkedIn, X, personal website):

_____
_____

If you find it challenging to answer these questions on your own, don't worry. You're not alone in this journey. Instead, consider reaching out to a diverse group of individuals for insight:

Ask 5 close friends and 5 coworkers the following question:
What are 2-3 things that you've learned from me that will bring value to others?

_____
_____
_____

This simple yet powerful question will provide valuable insights into how others perceive the value you bring. You may receive responses that confirm your expectations or surprise you with new perspectives. Either way, these answers will help you gain a clearer understanding of your personal brand and how you can effectively communicate and cultivate it on LinkedIn.

Once you have an understanding of your personal brand, share your strengths on LinkedIn and this time tell it like a story. Tell people that your coach Shantel Love encouraged you to do this reflection exercise to help you craft your personal brand, then ask your audience to share with you what their personal brand stands for.

This is a great opportunity to learn more about the people in your network, you are giving value by sharing your experiences, you now have a way to engage with your connections, and you may uncover partnership opportunities or your future client or job referral. This is a gift that just keeps on giving. Look at all that came from this one exercise.

THE CHALLENGES OF PERSONAL BRANDING

Let's have a heart-to-heart about this personal branding journey. You've likely heard the highlight reel—the success stories, the career leaps, the networking triumphs. But as your guide on this path, I owe you the full picture, including the challenges that lie ahead.

This isn't meant to discourage you. Rather, it's to arm you with the knowledge and resilience you'll need. Consider this your roadmap for the bumps and detours you might encounter.

In my years of coaching, I've seen patterns emerge—common hurdles that trip up even the most promising professionals. Let's shine a light on these challenges and, more importantly, equip you with strategies to overcome them.

So, grab a pen. Bookmark this section. Trust me, you'll find yourself returning to these insights time and time again as you navigate your personal branding journey.

The Challenges of Personal Branding

Imposter Syndrome

Let me reveal a hidden truth that often goes unspoken in the pursuit of success—a feeling that lingers in the background, casting doubt on even the most accomplished individuals. It's that unsettling notion that, despite your triumphs, you're merely pretending and could be unmasked at any moment. This is impostor syndrome, and it's far more widespread than you'd expect.

Imagine standing among accomplished peers, your resume gleaming with accolades, yet your heart races with fear of being unmasked as an impostor. It's a paradox: the higher you climb, the more intense this feeling becomes.

Even those who exude confidence battle this demon. It's the professional world's open secret, a shared struggle that, ironically, makes us feel isolated.

I've witnessed it in CEOs, rising stars, and felt it myself countless times. It's demoralizing and can make you question every achievement.

But remember this: feeling like an impostor doesn't make you one. Often, it's a sign you're growing, challenging yourself, and pushing boundaries. It's the shadow cast by your own brilliance.
The next time doubt creeps in, know you're part of a silent majority. Your achievements are real, your skills valuable, and your voice matters.

The Challenge: Feeling like a fraud despite your achievements.

- How to Overcome: Remember that everyone, even the most successful people, faces imposter syndrome at some point. Keep a brag book where you save compliments, positive feedback, and achievements. Reflect on these when doubt creeps in. Also, talk about your feelings with a mentor, coach, or therapist—they can offer perspective and reassurance.

Pressure and Scrutiny

The pressure to maintain a polished public image can be relentless in the digital age. Constant maintenance of your personal brand means regularly updating and adjusting how you present yourself professionally. This involves refreshing online profiles, creating new content, interacting with your audience, and adapting to changes in your field. It's an ongoing process that takes time and effort, but it keeps your brand current and accurately reflects your skills and goals.

Constant Maintenance: Keeping your personal brand up-to-date is ongoing and can be time-consuming.

- How to Overcome: Schedule regular updates to your LinkedIn profile, set aside time each week to engage with content, and plan your posts in advance. Tools like Taplio and Buffer can help you schedule posts so you're consistently active without feeling overwhelmed. Here is my Taplio link https://taplio.com/?via=shantel go give it a try.

- Also, write faster using an AI thought partner. There are many options out there but my personal favorite is Claud AI which can help you create a content calendar with content aligned to your niche and zone of genius.

Public Scrutiny: Increased visibility means more scrutiny and sometimes negative comments.

- How to Overcome: Develop a thick skin and focus on constructive feedback. Engage respectfully with critics and use negative feedback as an opportunity to learn and grow. Remember, not everyone will agree with you, and that's okay.

The Impact on Mental Health

While the benefits of personal branding are often highlighted, the toll it can take on mental health is rarely discussed. The pressure to constantly perform, the scrutiny of being in the public eye, and the comparison to others can lead to anxiety and stress.

Set boundaries for your online activities: Establish clear limits on when and how much time you spend managing your online presence.

- **Schedule digital detoxes:** Plan regular periods where you completely disconnect from digital devices and social media to recharge.
- **Take breaks when needed:** Listen to your body and mind, stepping away from brand maintenance tasks when you feel fatigued or stressed.
- **Practice mindfulness and seek professional help if you feel overwhelmed:** Incorporate mindfulness techniques into your routine and don't hesitate to consult a mental health professional if the pressure becomes too much.
- **Break your tasks into manageable chunks and focus on one aspect of your brand each week:** Divide your brand maintenance into smaller, achievable tasks and dedicate specific time to different elements of your brand on a rotating weekly basis.

Balancing Authenticity with Perception

Staying True vs. Expectations: There's often tension between staying true to yourself and meeting public expectations.

- How to Overcome: Identify three core values that are non-negotiable in your personal brand. Stick to these, no matter what. Authenticity is key to a sustainable personal brand. Engage with your audience in a way that feels natural to you, not forced.

Systemic Challenges

Bias and Discrimination: Despite your efforts, systemic bias and discrimination can still pose significant barriers.

- How to Overcome: Build a support network of allies and mentors who can advocate for you and provide guidance. Engage in communities that support diversity and inclusion. Use your platform to highlight and address these issues.

Unequal Opportunities: Not everyone has the same access to resources for building a personal brand.

In personal branding, unequal opportunities are a significant issue. Not everyone has the same access to resources, networks, or platforms needed to effectively build their brand. This inequality can reinforce existing disparities in professional success. As a personal branding mentor, I've seen these challenges firsthand, which motivated me get involved and create the Promote Your D@mn Self Community on LinkedIn.

How to Overcome: Leverage free or low-cost resources like LinkedIn's learning modules, webinars, local professional groups, and the Promote Your Damn Self community. Join organizations and attend events that focus on professional and/ or business development.

In my experience coaching clients, these challenges are common. For example, my client Maria, Director of Marketing, felt overwhelmed by the constant need to update her LinkedIn profile and engage with content. We worked together to create a manageable content and posting schedule, using tools to automate posts and setting realistic goals for engagement. My clients rarely post in real time as I encourage them to use scheduling tools like LinkedIn scheduler and Taplio. Feel free to use my link to check it out (https://taplio.com/?via=shantel).

Another client Tony, a Sales Professional, struggled with balancing authenticity and public expectations. We focused on defining his core values and integrating them into his personal brand strategy. This helped him stay true to himself while meeting professional expectations.

Building a personal brand is a complex, multifaceted process that goes beyond the surface-level tips often shared. By understanding and addressing these unspoken truths, you can create a personal brand that is not only successful but also sustainable and authentic. Remember, it's a marathon, not a sprint. Be patient, stay true to yourself, and keep evolving.

Think about it. You're not the same person you were ten years ago, right? If we are being honest, you're not even the same person you were this morning. We're constantly evolving, learning, growing. It's wild when you really stop to think about it

For so long, it's felt like you've been living according to everyone else's expectations, contorting yourself to fit into a version of success that wasn't your own. It's exhausting, constantly trying to meet standards that don't reflect who you are. But there comes a time when you realize enough is enough. You choose to step into your authenticity, even if it feels risky. And with each step, the fear begins to fade, replaced by a newfound sense of freedom. You discover that the most powerful brand you can build is the one that reflects your true self, flaws and all.

Now, I'm not saying it's easy. There are still days when I doubt myself. But overall? I'm proud of how far I've come.

But here's the thing - and this is important, so pay attention. Your journey? It's not gonna look like mine. It's not gonna look like anyone else's. And that's the beauty of it. Your personal brand is gonna keep evolving, just like you are.

So here's my advice, for what it's worth: take some time to check in with yourself regularly. Ask yourself the tough questions. Are you being true to who you are? Are you proud of the person you're becoming? Don't be afraid to shake things up if the answer is no.

THINGS TO REMEMBER FROM THIS CHAPTER

Start with deep self-reflection

Identify your strengths, values, and passions. Use these to craft a killer personal brand statement that showcases your unique value proposition.

Your personal brand is your professional superpower, even as a 9-to-5er

It's not bragging; it's smart career management. Think of your LinkedIn profile as your personal Super Bowl ad - make it count!

Audit and align your online presence

Google yourself, review your social profiles, and gather feedback from friends and colleagues. Use this insight to shape how you present yourself on LinkedIn.

Share your brand story authentically.

Be yourself, engage with your network, and don't be afraid to evolve. Your brand is a journey, not a destination.

Prepare for challenges like imposter syndrome and public scrutiny.

Remember, you ARE the brand. Be kind to yourself, stay true to your values, and focus on providing value to your network.

THINGS TO REMEMBER FROM THIS CHAPTER

Taking Action: Start Now

- Let's get you started on building that personal brand on LinkedIn. Our friends at LinkedIn create a quick video to help you get started building your personal brand on LinkedIn. Follow this link to get started now.

- https://www.linkedin.com/learning/rock-your-linkedin-profile/showcase-your-accomplishments-with-work-experience. You will want to watch this video because it will act as a baseline going into the next few chapters so make sure you stop and watch this video. You will not regret it. And I promise that I will be right here waiting for you when you get back and we will pick up where we left off.

- After you watch this video create a post sharing what you learned and add hashtag:

#ShantelTaughtME!

YOUR NOTES:

Take a moment to reflect

YOUR NOTES:

Take a moment to reflect

WRITE YOUR SUCCESS STORY: BECOMING A THOUGHT LEADER ON LINKEDIN

Unleash Your Thought Leader ☑

What you will learn

Unlock the #2 overlooked secret in personal branding. Learn how to transform your seemingly ordinary experiences into compelling content that captivates your audience and establishes you as an industry thought leader.

WRITE YOUR SUCCESS STORY: BECOMING A THOUGHT LEADER ON LINKEDIN

In our journey through personal branding, we've explored the concept of mental wealth—the richness of our inner world. Next, we'll explore **Social Wealth—the #2 critical mistake often neglected in personal branding, despite its immense value in our hyper-connected era.** Social wealth represents the collective value derived from our network of relationships, both personal and professional. It's a powerful force that shapes careers, opens doors to unprecedented opportunities, and provides resilience in times of uncertainty.

The true power of social wealth lies in its compounding nature. Each meaningful interaction not only adds value directly but also has the potential to exponentially expand your network, creating a ripple effect of opportunities. In today's digital age, platforms like LinkedIn have become central hubs for cultivating and leveraging this wealth.

For marginalized communities, women, and people of color, social wealth is particularly transformative. Here are the top three ways it creates impact:

- **Breaking Systemic Barriers:** Social wealth provides access to opportunities often limited by discrimination or lack of representation. This is crucial because it directly addresses the root of inequality in professional settings. By opening doors that might otherwise remain closed, social wealth allows talented individuals to showcase their skills and advance their careers, ultimately leading to more diverse leadership and decision-making across industries.

- **Amplifying Diverse Voices:** Through social wealth, underrepresented individuals can increase their visibility and amplify their perspectives in their respective fields. This is vital because it brings fresh viewpoints to the forefront of industry discussions, leading to more inclusive innovation and problem-solving. When diverse voices are heard, it challenges the status quo and drives progress toward more equitable and effective solutions in business and society.

- **Creating Powerful Support Systems:** Social wealth enables the formation of invaluable support networks and safe spaces. These are essential because they provide a foundation of mentorship, advice, and emotional support crucial for navigating career obstacles specific to marginalized groups. These support systems not only help individuals overcome immediate challenges but also foster long-term resilience and success, creating a ripple effect that uplifts entire communities.

By leveraging personal branding and thought leadership, individuals from all backgrounds can strategically build their social wealth. This not only advances individual careers but also contributes to broader social change, gradually reshaping industries to be more diverse, equitable, and inclusive. Social wealth isn't just about what you can gain—it's also about what you can give. The most valuable networks are built on reciprocity and mutual benefit. As we navigate the complexities of modern careers, cultivating social wealth through personal branding and thought leadership isn't just advantageous—it's essential for personal success and societal transformation.

At the heart of building social wealth lies the power of thought leadership, particularly on platforms like LinkedIn. You might be wondering, "Who cares what I think?" It's time to silence that nagging voice of self-doubt. Whether you're a customer service representative with a decade of experience or a leader at a Fortune 500 company, or an entrepreneur, your insights matter. The truth is, the world is hungry for fresh perspectives, and you have unique value to offer.

According to an Edelman and LinkedIn study, 55% of decision-makers use thought leadership to vet potential collaborators. That's right—while you've been sitting on your brilliant ideas, more than half of the leaders out there are actively seeking fresh perspectives to guide their choices. This includes those with titles and those without. Thought leaders on LinkedIn aren't just collecting virtual high-fives; they're collecting opportunities. They're writing articles for Forbes and Medium, commanding stages around the world, and positioning their expertise to empower their clients.

Now before I get ahead of myself, let me pause to clarify the difference between personal branding and thought leadership because it can be a bit confusing at first:

- **Personal Branding** is the practice of marketing yourself, your career, and your expertise as a brand. It's how you present yourself to the world, encompassing your skills, experiences, and unique value proposition. Think of it as your professional identity—the image and reputation you cultivate in your industry.
- **Thought Leadership**, on the other hand, is a step beyond personal branding. It involves consistently delivering value to your audience through your expertise, insights, and innovative ideas. Thought leaders don't just participate in conversations; they lead them, shaping industry trends and influencing decisions.

While distinct, personal branding and thought leadership complement each other beautifully. Your personal brand forms the foundation upon which you build your thought leadership. As you share valuable insights and lead discussions, your thought leadership, in turn, strengthens and elevates your personal brand.

Consider the story of Meka, a finance expert who lost her job despite 15 years of dedication and 15 years of missing the majority of her kids lives due to work. Despite her expertise, Meka struggled to find new opportunities because she hadn't built a personal brand or established herself as a thought leader. Her story underscores the importance of not just being good at what you do but also being known for it.

Now, let's explore five powerful ways that thought leadership builds on your personal brand and allows you to "Promote Your Damn Self":

- **Increased Visibility and Recognition:** Thought leadership amplifies your personal brand by putting your ideas in front of a wider audience. When you consistently share valuable insights on LinkedIn, you're not just adding to the noise—you're positioning yourself as a go-to expert in your field.

- **Enhanced Credibility and Trust:** By providing thoughtful analysis and innovative solutions, you build credibility that goes beyond what a resume or LinkedIn profile can convey. This trust is a cornerstone of a strong personal brand.

- **Elevated Networking:** Thought leadership opens doors to high-level connections. When you're known for your ideas, you're more likely to attract the attention of industry leaders, potential clients, and collaborators.

- **Career Insurance:** Establishing yourself as a thought leader provides a form of career insurance. Even if you face setbacks like Meka did, your reputation and network can help you bounce back stronger.

- **Opportunity Magnet:** Thought leaders don't just wait for opportunities—they attract them. Speaking engagements, media appearances, and business opportunities often come knocking when you're recognized as a thought leader in your space.

- **Accelerated Personal Growth:** While many focus on the external benefits of thought leadership, one overlooked advantage is the profound impact it has on your own personal and professional development. The process of consistently researching, analyzing, and articulating your ideas forces you to deepen your understanding of your field. As you engage with others' perspectives and defend your viewpoints, you're constantly learning and refining your own expertise.

Thought leadership isn't reserved for CEOs or those with decades of experience. Even if you're early in your career, you have unique perspectives to offer. The key is to start where you are, with what you know.

On LinkedIn, this means consistently sharing valuable content, engaging in meaningful discussions, and building genuine connections. It's about using your profile not just as a digital resume but as a platform to showcase your expertise and insights.

As you embark on this journey, remember that becoming a thought leader is not about self-promotion for its own sake. It's about providing value, nurturing insights, and cultivating a community. It's about using your knowledge to illuminate paths for others. By embracing personal branding and thought leadership, you're not just enhancing your own career prospects—you're creating a ripple effect of opportunities and growth for those around you.

Get ready to experience social wealth. We're about to transform your LinkedIn game – and your career along with it.

Before we jump, just in case you skipped the end of the last chapter, I encourage you to watch a video from our friends at LinkedIn. I will add it here just in case, it is a good baseline that will carry you through the next few chapters of this book. Here you go: https://www.linkedin.com/learning/rock-your-linkedin-profile/showcase-your-accomplishments-with-work-experience.

Becoming a thought leader isn't a walk in the park. It takes time, effort, and a whole lot of persistence. With the right strategies, we can make this journey a lot smoother and more effective.

> **HERE ARE THE 7 STEPS TO PROMOTE YOUR D@MN SELF AS A THOUGHT LEADER ON LINKEDIN.**

Step 1: Define Your Niche:

You can't be everything to everyone, so don't try. What do you know and are able to talk about effortlessly? What do you get excited about at work? What's the one thing people frequently seek your advice on? Maybe it's innovative project management techniques, or perhaps you're a great at cross-functional team leadership, or you give great career advice. Whatever it is, claim it.

Action step: Write down three areas where you excel and feel passionate. Now, narrow it down to one. That's your focus.

Your niche is where your expertise, passion, and market needs intersect. To find your niche, answer these questions:

- What are you passionate about?
- What are you skilled at?
- What problems do you notice in your industry that you can solve?

Example:
- Profession: Digital Marketing Specialist
- Target Audience: Small business owners
- Specific Problem: Struggling to create effective online marketing campaigns
- Unique Approach: Using data-driven strategies to maximize ROI on a small budget

Instead of just telling you to imagine your niche, let's dig deeper. What specific problems can you solve? What unique perspective do you bring? Write these down. This is your foundation.

Template : Define Your Niche

As a [Your Profession], I empower [Target Audience] to [Specific Problem You Solve] by [Your Unique Approach].

Example:
As a Digital Marketing Specialist, I empower small business owners to create effective online marketing campaigns by using data-driven strategies to maximize ROI on a small budget.

Step 2: Optimize Your Profile:

Your LinkedIn profile is your digital storefront. It needs to scream "thought leader" from the time someone lays their eyes on it.

- Craft a headline that packs a punch. Instead of "Marketing Manager at XYZ Corp,
    - try "Revolutionizing B2B Marketing | Turning Data into Dollars | Speaker & Podcast Host

- Your about section? Make it pop. Tell your story, showcase your expertise, and don't be afraid to let your personality shine through. (Reference my about section for inspiration)

- Skills and recommendations matter. Curate them to align with your chosen niche.

- Use a high-resolution and high-quality headshot

Tip:

Sometimes it's just not possible to get the perfect shot. In that case, you can take pictures on your cellphone and put your phone setting in portrait mode. Another option is AI-generated professional headshots. I've tried TryitonAI.com and Secta.ai.com, and they both did a great job of capturing my ethnic features and short hair. Most other AI tools couldn't quite get it right, but these two made me proud. Take a look at my profile and tell me if you can figure out which images on my profile are AI-generated.

Template: Profile Headline

I'm a [Profession] with over [X years] of experience in [Industry]. I specialize in [Key Skills/Expertise] and am passionate about [Interest]. My mission is to [Your Mission]. If you're looking for [Service/Advice/Partnership], feel free to connect with me.

Example:
I'm a Digital Marketing Specialist with over 10 years of experience in helping small businesses thrive online. I specialize in data-driven marketing strategies that maximize ROI on tight budgets. My mission is to empower small business owners with the tools and knowledge they need to succeed in the digital landscape. If you're looking for tailored marketing advice or a strategic partnership, feel free to connect with me.

Step 3: Create Content that Reflects Your Brand:

This is where the rubber meets the road. Understanding your audience's needs plus consistent, high-quality content is your ticket to thought leadership. But here's the secret – you don't have to reinvent the wheel every time.

- Start with what you know. What insights do you have that others in your field might find valuable?

- Mix up your content types:

    - Articles, posts, videos, infographics – variety is the spice of LinkedIn life.

- Use the 5-3-2 rule:

For every 10 posts, 5 should be curated content from others, 3 should be your original content, and 2 should be personal, fun content that humanizes your brand.

Efficiency hack: Batch create content. Set aside a couple of hours each month to brainstorm and outline multiple pieces. It'll save you time and keep your content calendar full. Let me tease this out a bit for those that may not fully grasp the concept of high-value content.

High-value content is information that your audience finds extremely useful, actionable, and relevant. It often answers their pressing questions, solves specific problems, or provides insights that are not easily accessible. I tell my clients that are running a business to give away the "What" and sell the "How". It may feel like you are giving away all of your secrets however, if you position that [What-the problem is] and you sell the [How- how to solve it] you will position yourself as a value add to your potential clients and audience.

Here's how to determine what high-value content is:

- **Identify Pain Points:** Understand the challenges and questions your audience faces. This can be done through surveys, engaging in LinkedIn groups, or direct conversations. What are they up googling at 2 am in the morning?

- **Provide Solutions:** Offer clear, actionable solutions to these pain points. The more specific and practical, the better. This can be (consulting, coaching, speaking, workshops, advisory, eBook, physical book, worksheets, workbooks, journals, or exclusive podcasts, you get where I am going, right?)

Share Unique Insights: Leverage your unique experiences and insights to offer perspectives that others might not have considered.

Examples of High-Value Content:

Case Studies:
- Detailing how a particular strategy or solution was successfully implemented.

- **Newsletter:** LinkedIn members who subscribe to your newsletter are genuinely interested in your insights, leading to higher engagement rates. In fact, LinkedIn reports that members who engage with newsletters are 2.5 times more likely to become regular readers of your content.

  - **A regular newsletter:** Helps you stay top-of-mind with your audience without the pressure of daily posts. Consistency is key to building a loyal audience; even just a monthly newsletter can keep you relevant.
  - **SEO Benefits:** By strategically using keywords, your newsletter can improve your visibility not only on LinkedIn but also in search engine results. LinkedIn articles and newsletters are indexed by search engines like Google, which means the right keywords can extend your reach far beyond the LinkedIn platform.

Example Post:
How we increased a small business's online sales by 200% in 6 months with data-driven marketing strategies. [Link to case study]

- **How-To Guides:** Step-by-step instructions on how to accomplish something specific.

Step 4: Start a movement and Engage, Engage, Engage

LinkedIn offers powerful tools to attract opportunities, expand your influence, and establish yourself as a thought leader.

Create a LinkedIn group:

(Ex: Women in Tech, Looking for work)
- Focus on your ideal client or target audience. This is a space where your target audience can get resources from you and engage
- Post articles, white papers, and content that allow them to learn from you
- Share your story so that they can learn more about you and build trust
- Do Live events to share with your audience relevant content that bring them value

Once you start the movement, engage with the community

- Comment on others' posts with insightful additions, not just "Great post!"
- Encourage people to join your LinkedIn group and participate in discussions.
- Don't just connect – follow up. Send a personalized message to new connections, mentioning something specific from their profile.

Step 5: Leverage LinkedIn's Features

LinkedIn is constantly evolving, rolling out new features that can position you as a thought leader, even if you're just starting out. And the best part? You don't even need a fancy website to get the ball rolling.

- LinkedIn Live: Picture this - you, chatting live with your audience about the latest industry trends. It's like having your own TV show, but without the hair and makeup team. Host Q&A sessions or informal chats about industry trends. It's a fantastic way to show off your expertise and connect with your audience in real-time. Plus, it's way less intimidating than you might think.

- **LinkedIn Newsletter:** Remember those email newsletters you used to send (and maybe still do)? Well, LinkedIn's got its own version, and it's a game-changer. Start one to deliver regular insights to your followers. It's like having a direct line to your audience's inbox, but without the hassle of managing an email list. Talk about a win-win!

- **LinkedIn Polls:** Want to know what your network thinks about a hot topic? Or maybe you're trying to decide on your next blog post theme? Polls are your new best friend. They're great for engagement and gathering insights from your network. Plus, people love sharing their opinions - give them a chance, and watch the interactions roll in.

Pro tip: Set a recurring calendar reminder to check LinkedIn's latest features every month. Stay ahead of the curve.

Step 6: Collaborate and Network

No thought leader is an island. I know this is a tough concept for many, but hear me out. Once you find your niche, engage with others in that space. You might see them as competition, but their audience can become your followers if you show up as a brand authority. No one on LinkedIn is only interacting with your competition. Collaborate with others in your field.

- Co-author articles with colleagues or industry peers. This collaborative approach not only expands your network but also brings diverse perspectives to your content, making it more valuable to your audience.

- Interview experts for your LinkedIn posts or newsletter. By featuring insights from respected professionals, you enhance your own credibility and provide your followers with exclusive, high-quality information.
- Attend (virtual or in-person) industry events and share your takeaways on LinkedIn. This demonstrates your commitment to staying current in your field and provides valuable insights to followers who couldn't attend the events themselves.
- Engage with your competition's audience in the comments (their followers can become your followers and future clients). This strategy allows you to showcase your expertise in a neutral space and potentially attract new followers who are already interested in your industry.

Your peers on LinkedIn can easily go from strangers to partnerships.

Who are the top 5 influencers or communities in your field that you should connect with? One tool to find top influencers by expertise is Taplio. Try it out: https://taplio.com/?via=shantel

Template : Establishing Collaboration Opportunities

Hi [Creator's Name],

I hope this message finds you well. My name is [Your Name], and I've been following your work on [specific topic/industry] with great interest. Your recent [project/content] on [specific detail] particularly caught my attention.

I'm reaching out because I believe there's potential for an exciting collaboration between us. My background in [your expertise] complements your work in [their expertise], and I have an idea that could blend our strengths:

[Brief outline of your collaboration idea]

What sets this apart:
1. [Unique aspect of your proposal]
2. [How it aligns with their recent work or stated goals]
3. [Potential benefit or impact for both parties]

I've also noticed your interest in [specific topic they've mentioned], which aligns perfectly with [aspect of your work]. This shared passion could add an interesting dimension to our collaboration.

Would you be open to a brief call to discuss this further? I'm excited about the possibility of creating something innovative together.

Looking forward to your thoughts,
[Your Name][Your LinkedIn profile link/ website]

Step 7: Continuous Improvement, focusing on realistic goal-setting and sustainable engagement:

1. Set Realistic Goals:

What are your achievable goals for your thought leadership and personal brand? Be specific but kind to yourself.

Short-term (next 3 months):

_____
_____
_____

Long-term (next 1 year):

_____
_____
_____

2. Design Your Engagement Rhythm:

How often can you comfortably engage on LinkedIn?

_____
_____

What type of content feels authentic to you?

_____
_____

Remember: Quality over quantity. It's better to post thoughtfully once a week than to force daily content that doesn't reflect your true voice.

3. Leverage Tools and Time Management:

Which scheduling tool will you use (e.g., LinkedIn's native scheduler, Buffer)?

_____
_____
_____

Set aside a specific time each week for LinkedIn activities. When works best for you?

_____
_____
_____

4. Monitor and Learn:

Review your LinkedIn analytics monthly.

What posts resonate most with your audience? What's working? Not working?

Track your Data points monthly (E.g. top performing post, impression, connections, etc.,.)
 Note any trends in profile views or connection requests.

5. Seek Balanced Feedback:
(Gain a supportive community. Do not try to do this alone.)
 - Who can provide honest, constructive feedback on your brand?

_____
_____
_____

Now, let's address the elephant in the room – time. I get it. You're already juggling a million things, and now I'm asking you to add "LinkedIn thought leader" to your plate. It seems daunting, right? But here's the thing – it doesn't have to be.

Here are a few tools to Make Your LinkedIn Thought Leadership Journey easier and save you time:

Canva

Canva is a graphic design platform that allows you to create stunning visuals without being a professional designer.
How it saves time: With pre-made templates and an intuitive drag-and-drop interface, you can create professional-looking graphics in minutes instead of hours.

High-quality visuals make your content more engaging and shareable, increasing your reach and perceived professionalism.
Why use it: Visual content gets 94% more views than text-only content. By creating eye-catching infographics, quote cards, or slide decks, you're more likely to stop the scroll and get your ideas noticed.

Hootsuite or Buffer

These are social media management platforms that allow you to schedule posts in advance and track engagement.

Instead of logging in daily to post, you can batch-create content and schedule it for optimal times, freeing up your day-to-day schedule.

Consistent posting is key to thought leadership. These tools ensure you maintain a regular presence even when you're busy.

Hootsuite found that their users save an average of 6 hours per week on social media management. That's time you can reinvest in creating more in-depth content or engaging with your audience.

H.A.R.O. (Help a Reporter Out)

H.A.R.O. is a free platform that connects journalists seeking expert sources with professionals who can provide insights for their stories.

Instead of cold-pitching media outlets or paying for PR services, H.A.R.O. delivers relevant media opportunities directly to your inbox, allowing you to respond quickly to targeted queries.

By getting quoted in reputable publications, you gain third-party validation of your expertise. This media exposure boosts your credibility and expands your reach to new audiences.

Descript

Descript is an all-in-one audio/video editing tool that allows you to edit your content as easily as you'd edit a document.

Its transcription feature and text-based editing make the editing process much faster than traditional editors.

By making it easier to produce polished video and audio content, Descript helps you diversify your content types, appealing to different learning styles in your audience.

Video content is king on LinkedIn, with users 20 times more likely to share a video post than any other type of post. Descript makes video creation accessible, even if you're not a tech expert.

LinkedIn Sales Navigator

This is LinkedIn's premium tool for advanced search, lead generation, and network building.

It provides deeper insights into your network and industry, allowing you to quickly identify and connect with key players.

By helping you identify and engage with the right people, it amplifies your networking efforts and expands your sphere of influence.

Users report up to 5% higher win rates and 35% larger deal sizes. For thought leaders, this translates to more meaningful connections and potentially lucrative opportunities.

Lumen5

Lumen5 is an AI-powered video creation platform that turns blog posts or text into engaging videos.

It automatically suggests visuals and layouts based on your

text, dramatically reducing the time it takes to create video content.

By repurposing your written content into video format, you can reach a wider audience and reinforce your key messages across multiple mediums.

LinkedIn users are 3 times more likely to engage with video posts compared to text posts. Lumen5 makes it easy to tap into this engagement without a huge time investment.

Feedly

Feedly is a news aggregator that collects content from various sources based on your interests.

Instead of manually checking multiple sites, Feedly brings all relevant content to one place, making it easier to stay informed and find shareable content.

Staying on top of industry trends is crucial for thought leadership. Feedly ensures you're always in the know and ready to provide timely insights.

Curating and sharing relevant content is a key part of thought leadership. Feedly users report saving an average of 1-2 hours per day on content discovery.

Grammarly

Grammarly is an AI-powered writing assistant that checks for grammar, spelling, and style issues.

It catches errors as you write, eliminating the need for multiple proofreading passes.

Polished, error-free writing enhances your credibility and professionalism.

Studies show that poor grammar can negatively impact credibility. Grammarly ensures your ideas shine without being overshadowed by minor errors.

Calendly

Calendly is a scheduling tool that allows others to book time with you based on your availability.

It eliminates the back-and-forth of scheduling meetings, saving an average of 4 hours per week.

It makes you more accessible for networking, interviews, or collaborations, crucial activities for growing your thought leadership.

As your influence grows, so will demands on your time. Calendly helps you manage these efficiently while still remaining open and approachable.

It automatically suggests visuals and layouts based on your text, dramatically reducing the time it takes to create video content.

Remember, the goal isn't to use every tool, but to select the ones that best fit your workflow and goals. Start with one or two that address your most pressing needs. As you grow more comfortable, you can incorporate more tools to streamline your efforts.

Becoming a thought leader is about playing the long game. It won't happen overnight, and that's okay. Each post, each comment, each connection is a step forward. Those steps add up.

Thought leadership isn't about being perfect—it's about being consistent, authentic, and always providing value. Pick a strategy or two that resonates with you, use a tool that simplifies your process, and start putting yourself out there. Your unique insights and experiences will set you apart on LinkedIn.

Embrace the journey, learn from your audience, and refine your approach. Before you know it, you'll be the go-to expert in your field, opening doors to new opportunities. Keep pushing, keep sharing your insights, and keep being authentically you. Your perspective is valuable, and the world needs to hear it.

So, my friend, are you ready to step into your power as a thought leader? It's time to let your brilliance shine on LinkedIn. You've got this, and I'm cheering you on every step of the way.

THOUGHT LEADERSHIP CHECKLIST:

1. Content Creation and Sharing
    - Create or curate one piece of valuable content
    - Use Canva to create an eye-catching visual for your post
    - Proofread your content with Grammarly
    - Schedule posts using Hootsuite or Buffer

2. Engagement
    - Spend 15 minutes engaging with your network's content
    - Reply to comments on your posts
    - Connect with one new relevant professional

3. Learning and Staying Informed
    - Check Feedly for industry news and trends
    - Save interesting articles for future content ideas

Weekly Thought Leadership Checklist:

1. Content Planning
    - Plan content calendar for the upcoming week
    - Brainstorm ideas for longer-form content (articles, videos)

2. Networking
    - Schedule at least one networking call using Calendly
    - Engage in at least one LinkedIn group discussion

3. Analytics Review
    - Check LinkedIn analytics for top-performing content
    - Review Hootsuite or Buffer analytics for engagement patterns

4. Skill Development
    - Spend 1 hour learning a new tool or skill (e.g., video editing with Descript)

THINGS TO REMEMBER FROM THIS CHAPTER

Define your niche

Identify the intersection of your expertise, passion, and market needs. Create a clear statement that articulates who you are, who you serve, and how you solve specific problems.

Optimize your LinkedIn profile

Craft a compelling headline, write an engaging "About" section, and use a high-quality profile picture. Your profile is your digital storefront, so make it reflect your thought leadership.

Create high-value content

Focus on solving your audience's pain points through various content types (articles, posts, videos). Use the 5-3-2 rule for the content mix: 5 curated, 3 originals, and 2 personal posts out of every 10.

Engage actively and start a movement

Create a LinkedIn group focused on your niche, host live events, and consistently engage with your network. Remember, thought leadership is a dialogue, not a monologue.

Collaborate and network strategically

THINGS TO REMEMBER FROM THIS CHAPTER

Connect with influencers in your field, co-create content, join LinkedIn groups to learn and for support, and attend industry events. Use tools like Taplio to identify key players in your niche and reach out for collaborative opportunities.

By following these steps and embracing the mindset of a thought leader, you'll build a powerful personal brand on LinkedIn and unlock countless career opportunities. Now, let's embark on this exciting journey together and make your voice heard.

LET'S TAKE ACTION:

Define your niche and create your thought leadership statement using this template:

As a [Your Profession], I empower [Target Audience] to [Specific Problem You Solve] by [Your Unique Approach].

Take 10 minutes right now to fill this out. This statement will serve as the foundation for your personal brand and guide your content creation on LinkedIn.

YOUR NOTES:

Take a moment to reflect

YOUR NOTES:

Take a moment to reflect

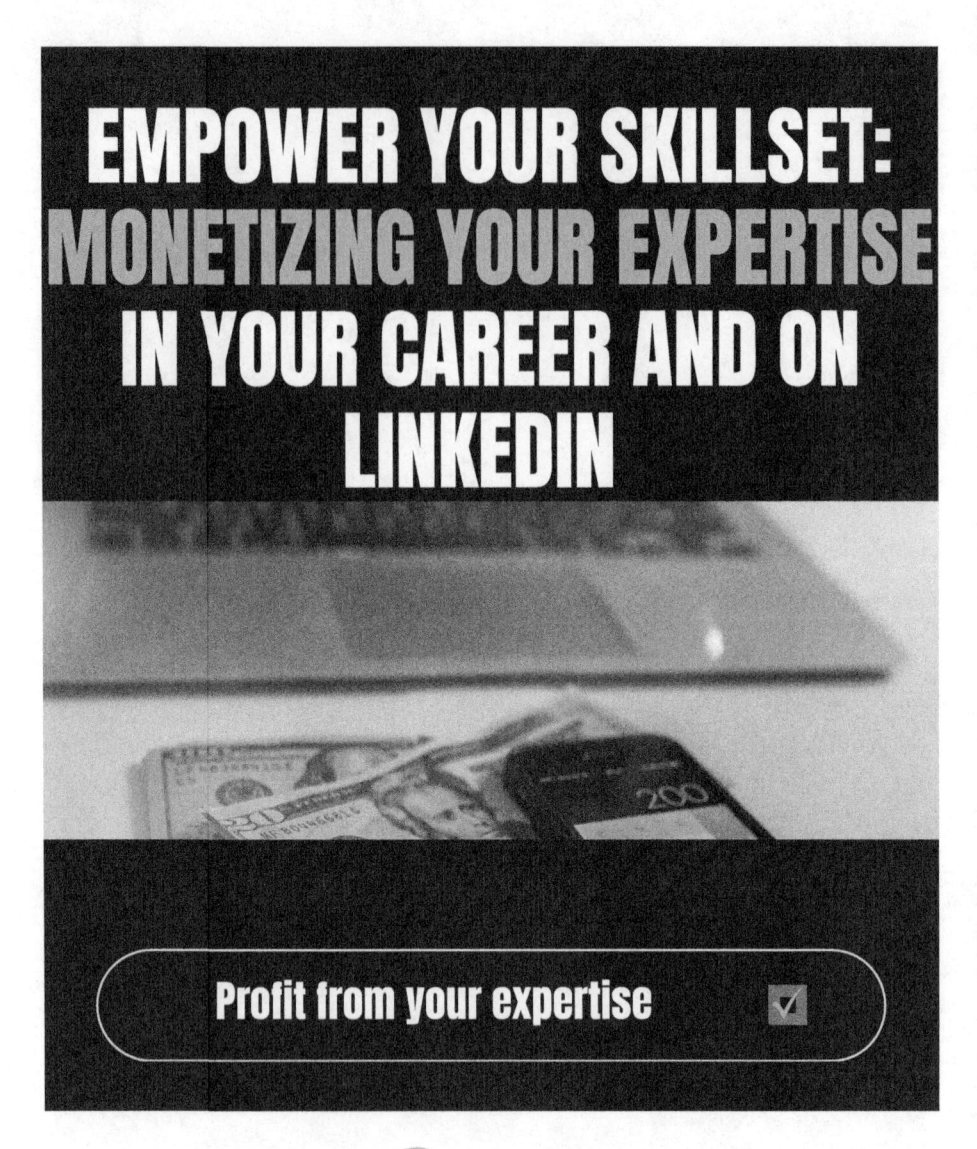

EMPOWER YOUR SKILLSET: MONETIZING YOUR EXPERTISE IN YOUR CAREER AND ON LINKEDIN

Profit from your expertise ✓

What you will learn

The #3 secret to personal branding unveiled: Turning influence into income. Master the art of monetizing your expertise, transforming your LinkedIn presence and day job into powerful revenue streams you never knew existed.

EMPOWER YOUR SKILLSET: MONETIZING YOUR EXPERTISE IN YOUR CAREER AND ON LINKEDIN

From sharpening your mind to expanding your network, we've been building towards this pivotal moment: maximizing your earning power and gaining financial wealth. But what exactly is financial wealth in the context of personal branding? It's more than just a hefty bank balance or a diversified investment portfolio. **Financial Wealth, the #3 mistake often underestimated in personal branding, is the art of converting your expertise, reputation, and network into concrete economic gains.** It's about elevating your personal brand beyond mere recognition to a lucrative asset—a crucial step many overlook in their personal branding journey.

By 2027, freelancers are projected to make up 50.9% of the total U.S. workforce (according to findings in the "Freelancing in America Study). A survey by Samsung and Morning Consult revealed that, 50% of Gen Z want to be their own boss. The future of work isn't just knocking; it's kicking down the door! This shift isn't just a trend; it's a seismic change in how we approach our careers and financial futures.

Your voice is currency in the attention economy—it's the currency that fuels your personal brand. It's your voice that distinguishes you, attracts others, and creates connections. Every time you express your truth, you're investing in your identity, revealing your value to the world. Monetization is simply the art of turning your insights into income.

I hear you loud and clear if you're a professional with a career and you're not looking to sell anything. The unfiltered reality is this: whether you realize it or not, you're selling something. The product?

You. Every day you walk into that office (or log into that Zoom call), you're selling. Selling your ideas in meetings. Selling your skills to your boss. Selling your value to the company. And if you're not actively selling yourself, you're leaving money on the table, plain and simple.

This isn't about becoming some pushy salesperson or turning your LinkedIn into a virtual billboard. It's about owning your worth and making sure everyone else knows it too. It's about turning your expertise into revenue-generating assets - bigger paychecks, juicier bonuses, and promotions that'll make your head spin.

Let me share a client story that'll light a fire under you. Ty, a sustainability expert and corporate employee, agreed to speak for free at a local business conference. He was nervous, thinking, "Who's gonna listen to me?" But he showed up and showed out. His passion was infectious. After his talk, three companies approached him for consulting opportunities. One of them turned into a six-figure contract. All from a freebie talk! The lesson? Sometimes, you gotta give to get. Your expertise is like a sample at Sam's Club - give people a taste, and they'll want the whole dang store.

Your LinkedIn profile isn't a resume; it's a billboard on the busiest highway of opportunities. Are you selling yourself short or showcasing your expert skills? Now, I know what you're thinking. "But I'm not an expert!" Stop right there. You've got years of experience, unique insights, and battle scars that are worth their weight in gold. It's time to own it.

Remember, monetization isn't always about cash upfront. It's about planting seeds that grow into money trees. That comment you left on a post? It could catch the eye of your next big client or recruiter. That article you shared? It might land you a speaking opportunity. If you stick with me all the way to the end of this chapter, I will share the exact strategies that I teach in my workshops and how my mentees and clients have gone from entry-level to executive roles and have 3x their income by leveraging the 3 types of wealth (mental, social, and financial). I promise you that you don't want to miss this.

Challenge: Start each day by asking yourself, what one action can I take today to create an opportunity for myself? Write it down and commit to doing it before the day ends.

Your career isn't just a job - it's a business. You are the CEO. It's time to start running it like one. Your financial wealth is waiting to be unlocked. All you need to do is turn the key. The future of work is here, and it's all about leveraging your unique voice and expertise. Let me tell you how.

The Power of Free

Now, I know what you're thinking. Free? I'm trying to make money here! Trust me on this one. Free can be your secret weapon. Let me tell you about my client, Lynn.

Lynn had been a corporate trainer and coach for almost 20 years but found herself stuck when it came to starting her own coaching business. She was passionate about wellness and dreamed of becoming a wellness coach, but the path forward wasn't clear to her.

When Lynn and I first started working together, she hired me to help her build her online business and personal brand. At the time, she was hesitant and unsure of where to start. She had the skills, the experience, and the passion, but she lacked the confidence to take the leap. The turning point came when I nudged her to take action. Lynn was a natural in front of groups, but the thought of posting videos online was intimidating. She worried about what people would think, if anyone would watch, and how she'd be received. I encouraged her to start small—just one video a week, with her face in it, talking about her passion for wellness. I also advised her to end each video with a call to action, inviting potential clients to reach out for a call if they want to work with her.

Her first few videos didn't get much traction. No likes, no comments, no messages. It was disheartening, to say the least. Lynn began to doubt herself and the process. But she didn't give up. She stayed consistent, kept posting, and continued to put herself out there.

On her fourth video, something amazing happened. A potential client from Europe reached out. Lynn, who was based in the US, was over the moon. She called me immediately, bursting with excitement and nerves. We role-played the breakthrough call she was going to have with this potential new client, preparing her to showcase her expertise and passion.

That call went better than either of us could have imagined. By the end of it, Lynn had booked her first client—a $5K six-week one-on-one coaching retainer. You read that right she made $5K and has never done this before as a coach but gives a way free advice on wellness daily. The joy and confidence that filled her voice were unforgettable. It was the validation she needed to believe in herself and her abilities.

Since then, Lynn's confidence has soared. She continues to work in her corporate job, but now she also coaches on the side. Her coaching business has grown, and she's even made enough money to buy a second home only working 10-15 hours a week doing her side hustle. The lesson? Free opportunities can be your foot in the door to paid opportunities. Lynn's story is a powerful reminder that sometimes the hardest step is just starting and that perseverance and consistency can lead to incredible opportunities.

Action Step: Identify one skill or piece of knowledge you can offer for free that provides immediate value to your target audience. Create a simple offer around it, like a free 15-minute consultation or a short video series.

Speaking Opportunities: Your Stage to Shine

It's not just about conquering stage fright - it's about conquering your financial future. Beside, if you are a leader or in a customer facing role then you are likely speaking in front of groups of people already sharing your expertise. 58% of buyers say an executive's ability to articulate value is crucial in their purchasing decisions. That's more than half your potential clients waiting to be wowed by your words. So why aren't you on that stage yet?

Even as a beginner, you could earn $500-$2,500 per speech. As you build your reputation, that could grow to $10,000 or more per engagement. As the great Tony Robbins once said, "The path to success is to take massive, determined action." Well, my friend, let's get you on that stage!

- **Start Local:** Look for local business groups, chambers of commerce, or industry meetups.

- **Leverage LinkedIn:** Use the search function to find events in your industry and start a video podcast or live events to get the footage and exposure.

- **Pitch Yourself:** Craft a compelling speaker proposal detailing the problem that you solve and the value that you can bring to their audience.

Template : Speaker Proposal

Subject: Unique Speaking Opportunity for [Event Name]

Dear [Organizer's Name],

I hope this email finds you well. I recently came across [Event Name] and was impressed by [specific detail about the event].

As a [your profession] with [X years] of experience in [your industry], I believe I can offer valuable insights to your audience on [proposed topic].

My talk, "[Catchy Title]," will cover:
- [Key Point 1]
- [Key Point 2]
- [Key Point 3]

After attendees hear me speak they will walk away with [specific, actionable takeaways].

I've attached my speaker bio and a short video clip of a recent talk I gave at [previous event].

I'm excited about the possibility of contributing to [Event Name]. Would you be open to a brief call to discuss this further?

Best regards,
[Your Name]

Action Step: Send out five speaking proposals this week. Remember, it's a numbers game!

Podcasts: Your Voice to the World

Not everyone's cut out for the written word. That's where podcasts come in. With over 2 million active podcasts out there, there's room for your voice. That's 2 million potential platforms for you to showcase your expertise.

It's like having your own radio show. Your expertise, your schedule, your rules. Get this you can also be a guest on a podcast if you are not interested in starting your own podcast. Most of my clients leverage the power of podcasts as guests to share their thought leadership, gain clients, and grow their businesses.

Here are a few tips to get you started.

1. Identify Relevant Podcasts:
   - Use tools like ListenNotes or PodcastGuests.com to find shows in your niche.
   - Listen to episodes to ensure your expertise aligns with the show's content.

2. Craft Your Pitch:
   - Personalize each pitch to the specific podcast.
   - Include potential topic ideas that would resonate with their audience.
   - Mention any previous media appearances or speaking engagements.

3. Prepare for Your Appearance:
- Research the host and recent episodes.
- Prepare talking points, but stay flexible for organic conversation.
- Have a quiet, echo-free space for recording.

4. Deliver Value During the Interview:
- Share actionable insights and real-world examples.
- Tell engaging stories that illustrate your points.
- Be authentic and let your personality shine.

5. Promote Your Appearance:
- Share the episode on your social media channels.
- Write a blog post expanding on topics discussed in the podcast.
- Include the appearance in your media kit or website.

6. Follow Up:
- Thank the host and offer additional resources for their audience if relevant.
- Stay in touch for potential future collaborations.

Monetizing Your Podcast Presence

- **Sponsorships:** As your audience grows, brands may want to reach them.
- **Affiliate Marketing:** Promote products or services you believe in.
- **Premium Content:** Offer exclusive episodes or content for paying subscribers
- **Consulting/Coaching:** Use your podcast to funnel listeners to your services.

- Create your on podcast: Newbies, could earn $500-$1,000 per month through sponsorships once you hit 5,000 to 10,000 downloads per episode.

Remember, podcasting is a marathon, not a sprint. Consistency and quality are key. Whether you're a host or guest, each episode is an opportunity to strengthen your personal brand, share thought leadership, and connect with your target audience. Embrace the power of your voice, and watch as doors open to new opportunities in your professional journey.

Template : Podcast Pitch

Subject: Unique Guest Idea for [Podcast Name]

Hi [Host's Name],

I'm a long-time listener of [Podcast Name] and particularly enjoyed your recent episode on [specific episode]. Your discussion on [particular point] really resonated with me.

I thought your audience might be interested in exploring [related topic]. As a [your profession] with [X years] of experience, I've [your unique perspective or achievement].

I'd love to share insights on:
- [Talking Point 1]
- [Talking Point 2]
- [Talking Point 3]

These insights have helped my clients [specific, impressive result]. I believe your audience would find immense value in this discussion.

I've attached a short audio clip introducing myself and the topic. Would you be interested in exploring this further?

Looking forward to hearing from you,

[Your Name]

> **ACTION STEP: PITCH YOURSELF TO THREE PODCASTS THIS WEEK. REMEMBER, CONSISTENCY IS KEY!**

Writing a Book: Your Thoughts, Immortalized

Writing a book is a powerful way to establish yourself as an authority in your field and leave a lasting impact. It's not just about personal fulfillment; it's a strategic business move that can open doors to new opportunities and significantly boost your professional profile. Expect to earn 10-15% of the list price in royalties for print books, and 25% or more for eBooks. For a $20 book, that's $2-$3 per copy sold.

The Business Impact:

The statistic mentioned (96% of business owners seeing a boost after writing a book) underscores the tremendous potential of authorship. A book can:
- Enhance your credibility and expert status
- Generate leads and attract new clients
- Serve as a high-value business card
- Create additional revenue streams
- Open doors to speaking engagements and media appearances

Your 24/7 Salesperson:

Unlike other marketing tools, a book works round the clock to promote your ideas and services. It can reach people you might never meet in person, extending your influence far beyond your immediate network.

Getting Started:

Choose Your Topic:
- Identify your area of expertise
- Consider what problems you can solve for your target audience
- Look for gaps in existing literature that you can fill
- Think about unique experiences or insights you can share

Create an Outline:
- Start with a broad structure (introduction, main chapters, conclusion)
- Break each chapter into key points or subsections
- Consider including case studies, exercises, or actionable tips
- Ensure a logical flow of ideas throughout the book

Set a Writing Schedule:
- The 500-words-a-day goal is an excellent starting point
- Find your most productive time of day for writing
- Create a dedicated writing space
- Use tools like timers or writing software to stay focused

Consider Self-Publishing:
- Platforms like Amazon KDP, IngramSpark, or Lulu offer accessible options
- Research the pros and cons of traditional vs. self-publishing
- Consider leveraging AI or hiring an editor and designer for a

- professional finish
- Plan your marketing strategy well before publication

Additional Considerations:
- Research your target audience to ensure your content meets their needs
- Consider incorporating multimedia elements (e.g., QR codes linking to videos)
- Think about companion products or services to offer alongside your book
- Plan for updates or new editions to keep your content relevant

Overcoming Challenges:
- Deal with writer's block by freewriting or changing your environment
- Seek feedback from peers or beta readers
- Stay motivated by visualizing your end goal and the impact your book will have

Remember, writing a book is a journey. It requires persistence and dedication, but the potential rewards – both personal and professional – can be immense. Your book is not just a collection of words; it's a legacy that can continue to generate value and impact lives long after it's published.

Template : Structuring Your Book

1. Introduction: Your journey and why this topic matters
2. Chapter 1: The basics everyone needs to know
3. Chapter 2: Common challenges and solutions

4. Chapter 3: Advanced tips and tricks
5. Conclusion: Call to action and next steps

> **ACTION STEP: WRITE THE OUTLINE FOR YOUR BOOK TODAY. JUST START!**

The e-learning market is set to hit $375 billion by 2026. That's a billion with a 'B'. Want a piece of that pie? Start baking. Create online courses, webinars, or master classes. Share your knowledge, and watch your bank account grow. Here's how you can get your slice of the pie:

1. **Identify Your Audience's Pain Points:** What problem can you solve?
   - Conduct market research to understand your target audience's needs
   - Use surveys, social media polls, or forums to gather insights
   - Analyze competitors to find gaps in the market you can fill

2. **Create a Course Outline:** Break your solution into digestible modules.
   - Start with an introduction and end with a conclusion
   - Organize content logically, building on previous concepts
   - Include practical exercises, quizzes, and assignments to reinforce learning

3. **Choose a Platform:** Consider Teachable, Udemy, or Thinkific.
   - Compare features, pricing, and user experience
   - Look for platforms that offer marketing tools and analytics
   - Consider creating your own website for complete control and branding

4. **Price Strategically:** Start with a lower price to gather

testimonials, then increase.
 - Research competitor pricing to position your course effectively
 - Consider offering tiered pricing options (e.g., basic, premium, VIP)
 - Implement launch discounts or early bird specials to drive initial sales

5. **Develop High-Quality Content:**
   - Invest in good equipment for professional-looking videos and clear audio
   - Create engaging visuals, such as infographics or animations
   - Provide supplementary materials like workbooks or checklists

6. **Market Your Course:**
   - Leverage social media platforms to build buzz
   - Create a lead magnet (e.g., free mini-course) to grow your email list
   - Collaborate with influencers or affiliates in your niche

7. **Gather and Implement Feedback:**
   - Encourage students to leave reviews and testimonials
   - Use feedback to continuously improve your course
   - Consider creating advanced or specialized courses based on student demand

8. **Provide Excellent Student Support:**
   - Respond promptly to questions and concerns
   - Create a community forum for students to interact and support each other
   - Offer office hours or live Q&A sessions for personalized assistance

9. **Stay Updated and Refresh Content:**
   - Regularly update your course to keep information current
   - Add new modules or bonuses to increase value over time
   - Stay informed about industry trends and incorporate them into your teachings

By following these steps and continuously refining your approach, you can create a successful online course that not only generates income but also provides real value to your students.

Template : Structuring Your Course

Module 1: Introduction and Overview
- Define your target audience and their pain points
- Outline the benefits of your offer and what sets it apart

Module 2: Core Principles and Foundations
- Describe the core principles or methodologies underlying your offer
- Identify key features and components that make up your offer

Module 3: Practical Applications and Case Studies
- Provide examples or case studies demonstrating how your offer solves real-world problems
- Detail the outcomes or results clients can expect from your offer

Module 4: Advanced Techniques
- Explore advanced techniques or customization options available
- Discuss potential upgrades or additional services to enhance your offer

Module 5: Final Project and Certification
- Outline any final project or assignment participants can complete to apply what they've learned
- Offer a certification or recognition upon successful completion of the course or program

> **ACTION STEP: SURVEY YOUR NETWORK ABOUT THEIR BIGGEST CHALLENGES RELATED TO YOUR EXPERTISE. USE THIS TO INFORM YOUR COURSE CONTENT.**

Creating Worksheets and Resources

Feeling overwhelmed? Start small. Create worksheets or resources. They can be freebies to build your email list or paid products to start that cash flow. Sometimes, a full course might feel like too much of a lift. That's okay! Start with creating worksheets or other resources that can serve as freebies or paid products. Here's a template to help you get started:

Worksheet: Creating Your Offer

1. **Identify Your Expertise**
   - What skills or knowledge do you have that others find valuable?

2. **Define Your Audience**
   - Who can benefit the most from your expertise?

3. **Choose Your Medium**
   - How will you deliver your knowledge (eBook, workshop, course)?

4. **Outline Your Offer**
What will your offer include? (Chapters, modules, sections)

5. **Create a Marketing Plan**
How will you promote your offer? (Social media, email lists, webinars)

6. **Set Your Goals**
What do you want to achieve with this offer? (Sales, brand awareness, leads)

Action Step: Fill out this worksheet for an offer you'd like to create. This could be anything from a free PDF guide to a paid consulting package.

MONETIZING YOUR CAREER

Imagine a world where your expertise isn't just respected—it's your ticket to financial freedom. A world where the color of your skin or the pronouns you use don't determine your paycheck. Sounds too good to be true? We're about to flip the script on the wage gap narrative and show you how to transform your career into one of your biggest opportunities.

On average, women earn 82 cents for every dollar a man makes. Black women? 63 cents. Latina women? A measly 55 cents. It's not just pennies we're talking about—it's dreams deferred, opportunities lost, and potential squandered.

Want to know how long it takes a woman to earn what a man makes in a year? Mark your calendars for March 15th—that's 2.5 extra months of work. For Black women, it's August 3rd. Latina women? October 5th. It's not just a gap; it's a chasm.

Now, I know what you're thinking. "This is depressing as hell." And you're right. But here's where we change the game.
While we can't single-handedly fix a broken system overnight, we can sure as hell build a bridge over it. And that bridge? It's called monetizing your expertise.

Picture this: You're a marketing specialist, underpaid and underappreciated at your 9-to-5. But by night, you're running a thriving side hustle, teaching small businesses how to crush it on social media. Average earnings for a marketing consultant side opportunity? $50-$150 per hour. Suddenly, that wage gap is looking a lot less intimidating, isn't it?

Or maybe you're a software engineer, tired of watching less qualified colleagues zoom past you on the corporate ladder. So you start a coding bootcamp for kids in your community. Online tutors can easily rake in $30-$100 per hour. Or you are a customer service representative, you feel stuck in your career. So you blend your customer service experience with your passion for baking and you start a business baking goods for your community bringing in $100-$500 each week. That's not just extra cash—that's economic empowerment.

Are you aware that, Black women are the fastest-growing group of entrepreneurs in the U.S., with a 164% increase between 2007 and 2018. They're not waiting for permission—they're creating their own tables and pulling up their own chairs.

Take Reina, a Latina HR professional who started a resume writing service on the side. Within a year, she was making more from her "hobby" than from her day job. Or Aisha, a Black woman in tech who launched a YouTube channel sharing coding tips. She now earns six figures from ad revenue and sponsorships alone.

These aren't just success stories—they're blueprints for revolution. By monetizing your expertise, you're not just supplementing your income; you're reclaiming your worth. You're saying, "If you won't pay me what I'm worth, I'll Promote My D@mn Self to CEO and create my own damn paycheck."

Now, let's talk about your corporate currency. It's like a blank check – if you don't cash it in, you're literally leaving money on the table. Are you ready to make that deposit, or are you cool with watching your worth collect dust?

Your corporate currency isn't just some fluffy concept – it's the lifeblood of your career advancement and financial freedom. It's everything you bring to the table: your skills, your knowledge, your network, your reputation. And if you're not actively investing and spending this currency, you're not just stagnating – you're actively losing value. If you need help figuring that out feel free to reach out to me or check out one of the ways I can support you.

Every time you shy away from negotiating your salary, you're tearing up a paycheck. Every time you pass on a challenging project, you're shredding an opportunity for growth. When you skip that training session or ignore that LinkedIn connection request, you're flushing potential down the drain.

Your corporate currency isn't limited to your 9-to-5. It's a 24/7 asset that can be converted into financial freedom through side hustles, speaking opportunities, consulting jobs, and more. That presentation you nailed last week? That's not just a win for your current job – that's material for a phenomenal workshop you could be selling to other professionals. The process you streamlined in your department? That's a consulting opportunity waiting to happen. (**CAVEAT:** *If you just jumped into the chapter and skipped past the others go back to the chapter on Navigate LinkedIn Confidently: Thriving Under Your Boss's Watchful Eye to learn about transparency with your employer and HR, it is important to CYA, understand your companies policies so that you do not put your job at risk by unintentionally creating a conflict of interest*).

Let's break this down so that you can understand where your career currency and financial wealth opportunities lie.

Salary Negotiations: A $5,000 bump in your salary today could lead to over $600,000 more in your lifetime income. That's nothing to scoff at

Learning and Development: Employees who spend 5 hours a week learning are 47% less likely to be stressed, 39% more likely to feel productive and successful, 23% more ready to take on additional responsibilities, and 21% more likely to feel confident and happy. That's not just career advancement – that's life improvement.

Speaking Engagements: Even starting out, you can make $500 to $2,500 per speech. As your name becomes known, that can increase to $10,000 or more per event.

Consulting: The average consultant earns between $61,000 to $140,000 per year. That's a pretty sweet side opportunity, wouldn't you say?

Your expertise is like a muscle. The more you use it, the stronger it gets. And the stronger it gets, the more valuable it becomes. So every time you flex that corporate currency - whether it's by pitching a new idea at work, creating content on LinkedIn, or launching a weekend workshop - you're not just making money. You're compounding your worth.

Let me share a story about Zoe, a sales rep at a fast-growing SaaS company. She was crushing it, consistently hitting her targets. But when she found out she was pregnant, she worried about how it would impact her career trajectory.

During her maternity leave, Zoe did something that changed everything. Instead of completely disconnecting, she used some of her downtime to share her sales insights on LinkedIn. Nothing fancy—just quick posts about client communication tips or how she handled objections. She even wrote a couple of longer articles about balancing new motherhood with a sales career.

What Zoe didn't realize was that her content was catching the eye of not just her peers, but also the higher-ups at her company. They saw a side of Zoe they hadn't before—someone with leadership potential who could articulate sales strategies clearly.

When Zoe returned from maternity leave, she was surprised to find herself in conversations about a newly created sales leadership role. The company had been impressed by her thought leadership during her time away and saw her as the perfect fit to lead and mentor the growing sales team.

Zoe took the leap, and it paid off big time. She gained equity in the company, a performance-based bonus structure, travel perks, access to advanced resources, and most importantly, influence in major company decisions.

Zoe found that her new role actually gave her more flexibility to balance work and family life. She could delegate tasks, work on strategic projects from home, and set an example for other parents in the company.

Zoe's story isn't about working herself to the bone. It's about recognizing opportunities to add value, even when life throws you a curveball. By sharing her expertise and staying engaged (on her own terms) during a major life transition, Zoe opened doors she never knew existed.

Now, let's talk about your LinkedIn monetization gameplan, inspired by Zoe's success:

Strategic Visibility: Make your profile work for you 24/7. Use a professional photo (increases views by 21x), craft a compelling headline that showcases your unique value proposition, and if you have an offer or service invite people to work with you.

Authentic Engagement: Build relationships, not just connections. Provide thoughtful comments on posts in your field, participate actively in industry-specific LinkedIn groups, and engage with your company's content to increase internal visibility.

Strategic Network Expansion: Focus on quality over quantity. Connect with industry leaders and decision-makers, build cross-departmental relationships within your company, and leverage alumni networks for diverse industry perspectives.

Skill Showcase: Let your expertise shine. Regularly update your skills section with newly acquired competencies, seek endorsements from colleagues and clients for key skills, and offer genuine endorsements to strengthen professional relationships.

Thought Leadership: Position yourself as an industry innovator.

Share your unique perspective on industry challenges, create content that bridges your professional and personal experiences, and don't shy away from discussing how you navigate career transitions.

Opportunity Alertness: Be ready for the next big step. You don't have to get ready if you stay ready. Keep your career goals updated in your profile, use LinkedIn's "Open to Work" feature strategically, and engage with posts from companies you're interested in.

Your career path isn't always linear. Sometimes, the moments you think might slow you down can actually catapult you forward —if you approach them strategically.

So, are you ready to stop leaving stacks of cash on the table? Are you prepared to turn your knowledge into cold, hard cash in your paycheck, whether that's through raises, promotions, or juicy bonuses?

It's time to reframe your perspective. Your knowledge isn't just a tool for your job - it's a powerful asset that can and should be leveraged for your financial benefit. Whether you're ascending the corporate ladder or building your own venture, the time to monetize your expertise is now.

The world is waiting for what you have to offer. It's time to stop hiding your light and start illuminating the path to your financial freedom. Your blank check is waiting – all you need to do is fill in the amount. Are you ready to cash in on your corporate currency and write your own success story?

Turn the page for templates and strategies to get you going. We will start will with building up your LinkedIn recommendations.

Template : Reaching Out For LinkedIn Recommendations

Hi [Name],

I hope you're doing well! I'm reaching out to ask if you would be willing to write a recommendation for me on LinkedIn.
Over the past [mention time frame or specific projects], we've had the opportunity to work together on [highlight specific tasks, projects, or roles]. Your insights and collaboration have been invaluable to me, and I believe your perspective would add significant value to my LinkedIn profile.

If you're comfortable with it, I'd love for you to highlight [mention specific skills, qualities, or achievements you'd like them to focus on, e.g., leadership, problem-solving abilities, customer focus, adaptability]. Of course, please feel free to mention anything else you feel is relevant.

Here's a quick summary to help guide you:
- Project/Role: [Briefly describe your role or the project you worked on together]
- Key Achievements: [Mention 2-3 specific outcomes or achievements]
- Skills to Highlight: [List the key skills or attributes you'd like them to mention]

I know how busy you are, so I genuinely appreciate your time and support in writing this. It would mean a lot to me to have your endorsement.

Thank you so much for considering this, [Name]. If you need any more details or have any questions, please don't hesitate to ask.
Best regards,
[Your Name]

Transforming your LinkedIn presence into tangible financial gains requires more than just networking; it's about strategically positioning yourself for lucrative opportunities. By enhancing your visibility, you can attract internal promotions or exciting new roles as your profile showcases your expertise to decision-makers. Externally, a compelling LinkedIn profile can capture the attention of recruiters, leading to job offers that may surpass your current position in both responsibility and compensation.

For those aiming even higher, demonstrating leadership and industry insight on LinkedIn can pave the way to coveted board positions, offering substantial compensation and expanding your professional network. In this context, every interaction on LinkedIn becomes an investment in your future, as you strategically build a personal brand with significant financial potential.

Here's a groundbreaking tip that'll set you apart:

Create a "Value Vault."

This is a document where you track every win, every problem solved, every dollar saved or earned for your company. Update it weekly. When it's time for your performance review or you're eyeing a new role, you've got a goldmine of data to back up your value.

Let me leave you with this thought:

Your expertise is your currency in the knowledge economy. Every day you're not showcasing it is a day you're leaving money on the table. So get out there and promote your damn self. Your bank account will thank you.

Remember, in the words of the great Estée Lauder, "I never

dreamed about success. I worked for it."

And if you are trying to figure out strategies on how to monetize your internal network at work. I got you. It starts with you.... Selling yourself. Whether you like it or not, you're in sales. The product? Your Amazing self.

Every day you walk into that office (or log into that Zoom call), you're selling. Selling your ideas in meetings. Selling your skills to your boss. Selling your value to the company. And if you're not actively selling yourself, you're leaving money on the table, plain and simple.

Let's talk about something that's often overlooked: your internal network. Sure, everyone's raving about LinkedIn and external networking, but the real treasure trove is right under your nose.

According to a study by Payscale, 70% of all jobs are not even published publicly. That's right, 7 out of 10 jobs are filled through internal networking. So, let's get you plugged in!

Internal Networking Strategy:

- **Coffee Roulette:** Set up a system where you have coffee with a random colleague from a different department each week. This expands your internal network and gives you insights into other areas of the company.

- **Cross-Departmental Projects:** Volunteer for projects that involve multiple departments. This showcases your skills to a wider audience within your company.

- **Internal Newsletter Contribution:** If your company has an internal newsletter, offer to write articles showcasing your expertise. This positions you as a thought leader within the organization.

Template: Internal Networking Email

Subject: Quick coffee catch-up?

Hey [Colleague's Name],

I hope this email finds you well. I've been really impressed with the work your team's been doing on [specific project]. I'd love to grab a quick coffee and learn more about your role and the challenges you're tackling.

Do you have 15 minutes this week? I'm free on [suggest 2-3 time slots].

Looking forward to connecting!

[Your Name]

Now, let's talk about something that'll make your boss's jaw drop: reverse mentoring. Yeah, you heard that right. Forget waiting for a mentor; become one instead, even to those above you on the corporate ladder.

Reverse Mentoring Strategy:
1. Identify Your Unique Skills: What do you know that older colleagues might not? Social media trends? Latest tech? Gen Z insights?
2. Pitch the Idea: Approach senior colleagues or your boss with the concept of skill exchange.
3. Set Clear Objectives: What will they learn? What will you gain?

Template : Pitch Reverse Mentoring

Subject: Innovative Skill Exchange Proposal

Dear [Senior Colleague's Name],

I hope this email finds you well. I've been reflecting on our company's commitment to innovation and continuous learning, and I have a proposal that I believe could benefit both of us and the company as a whole.

I'd like to suggest a reverse mentoring arrangement where I could share my expertise in [your area of expertise, e.g., social media trends, Gen Z consumer behavior] while learning from your vast experience in [their area of expertise, e.g., strategic decision-making, leadership].

Here's what I propose:
- Bi-weekly 30-minute sessions
- Alternating topics between your expertise and mine
- Clear learning objectives for each session

I believe this exchange could bring fresh perspectives to our work and foster innovation. Would you be open to discussing this further?

Looking forward to your thoughts,
[Your Name]

Now, let's talk about something that'll really set you apart: becoming the company's futurist. Yeah, you heard me right. Every company needs someone who can see around corners, and that someone could be you.

Becoming the Company Futurist:

- Start a "**Future Trends**" newsletter within your company. Share insights on industry trends, emerging technologies, and potential disruptors.
- Host monthly "**Future Friday**" sessions where you present a potential future scenario and facilitate a discussion on how it could impact the company.
- Create a "**Future-Proofing**" proposal for your department or the entire company.

Here's a mind-bending quote for you from Alvin Toffler: "The illiterate of the 21st century will not be those who cannot read and write, but those who cannot learn, unlearn, and relearn." That's your mantra now, my friend.

Now, here's a groundbreaking tip that no one's talking about: Create your own job title. Yeah, you heard me right. Don't wait for a promotion or a new role to open up. Craft a role that showcases your unique skills and aligns with the company's future needs.

Creating Your Own Job Title:

- **Identify the Gap:** Thoroughly analyze what's missing in your company that you could effectively fill with your unique skills and experience. Look for unmet needs or untapped opportunities.
- **Craft the Title:** Create a clear, compelling, and future-focused job title that accurately reflects the role and its importance. Ensure it aligns with industry standards while highlighting its unique aspects.
- **Write the Job Description:** Outline comprehensive

responsibilities, required skills, and qualifications. Clearly articulate how this role will benefit the company, including potential impact on efficiency, innovation, or growth. Include both essential and preferred qualifications.
- **Create a 90-day Plan:** Develop a detailed roadmap showing what you'd achieve in this new role during the first three months. Include specific goals, milestones, and metrics for success. Demonstrate how you'll quickly add value and integrate into the organization.

Template: Proposing Your New Role:

Subject: Innovative Role Proposal - [Your Proposed Title]

Dear [Boss's Name],

I hope this email finds you well. As we continue to evolve and adapt to the changing business landscape, I've identified an opportunity for a new role that I believe could significantly benefit our team and the company as a whole.

Proposed Title: [Your Proposed Title, e.g., Digital Transformation Catalyst]

Role Overview: [Brief description of the role and its importance]

Key Responsibilities:
1. [Responsibility 1]
2. [Responsibility 2]
3. [Responsibility 3]

Benefits to the Company:
1. [Benefit 1, e.g., Accelerated digital adoption across departments]
2. [Benefit 2, e.g., Improved cross-functional collaboration]

Benefit 3, e.g., Increased innovation output]
- *I've attached a detailed 90-day plan outlining specific objectives and deliverables for this role.*

I'm excited about the potential impact of this position and would love to discuss it further. Are you available for a 30-minute meeting next week to explore this idea?

Looking forward to your thoughts,
[Your Name]

Remember, my friend, your career is not a ladder; it's a jungle gym. Sometimes you need to move sideways or even backwards to position yourself for a big leap forward.

I had a client, let's call him Sean. He was stuck in middle management, watching others get promoted over his. Instead of waiting for an opportunity, he created one. He noticed the company was struggling with employee engagement. So, he started an unofficial "Culture Club," organizing events and initiatives to boost morale. He tracked the impact: increased productivity, decreased turnover. After six months, he presented his results to the C-suite and pitched a new role: Chief Culture Officer. Guess who's now sitting in the executive meetings? That's right, our guy Sean.

The lesson? Don't wait for the perfect role to come along. Create it.

Now, let's talk about money. Here's a stat that'll make your head spin: According to a study by Salary.com, 37% of employees always negotiate their salary, while only 44% negotiate occasionally. That means more than half of employees are leaving money on the table. Don't be one of them.

- **Know Your Worth:** Research market rates on Payscale. Network for insider insights, talk to those that are doing the job that you want . Every $5,000 salary increase now could mean $600,000+ over your career.
- **Quantify Your Impact:** Detail concrete contributions that you made to the bottom line. Use specific metrics, percentages, and dollar amounts. Highlight efficiency improvements, cost savings, and revenue generation.
- **Think Beyond Salary:** Consider the full compensation package: This may include performance bonuses, signing bonuses, stock options or equity, retirement plans, health benefits, professional development budgets, flexible working arrangements, additional paid time off, etc,.
- **Learning and Development:** Employees who spend 5 hours a week learning are 23% more ready to take on additional responsibilities.

Template: Negotiation Conversation

Thanks for meeting with me to discuss my compensation. Over the past year, I've [list 2-3 major achievements with quantifiable results]. Based on my research and the value I bring to the company, I believe a salary of [your target number] would be appropriate. I'm also open to discussing other forms of compensation such as [list 2-3 other benefits you're interested in]. How can we work together to make this happen?

Your personal brand is your secret weapon you have to vocalize your value. It's not just about what you do; it's about how you're perceived. Are you the problem solver? The innovator? The peacemaker? Figure out your unique value proposition and shout it from the rooftops (or at least from your cubicle).

Here's a groundbreaking tip: Create a personal brand board of directors. Just like companies have a board to guide them, you need your own personal board. These are 3-5 people who know you, believe in you, and will give you honest feedback. Meet with them quarterly to review your career goals and strategies.

Lastly, remember this: Your career is a marathon, not a sprint. As the great Muhammad Ali said, "Don't count the days, make the days count." Every day is an opportunity to build your brand, expand your network, and increase your value.

Let me tell you a story about Trina, and trust me, her journey is going to blow your mind.

Trina's a sales rep, a total BOSS in education policy. We're talking top university grad, quota-crushing royalty, with enough swagger to make even the toughest negotiators weak in the knees. This woman was the undisputed queen of sales for a solid decade, hopping from one company to another, leaving a trail of blown quotas and impressing clients in her wake.

But here's the thing- despite all her success, Trina was stuck. She had this dream of becoming a VP. Not just for herself, but to show her little girl what a boss lady looks like. But for all her sales expertise, when it came to selling herself? Crickets.

I'm sitting across from Trina in one of our coaching sessions and

I can see it in her eyes. She's got that fire, that hunger. So I look her dead in the eye and say, "Trina, girl, it's time to apply for that VP role."

You should've seen her face. It was like I'd suggested she walk on water. But here's the thing about Trina - she's got guts. So she goes for it... well, sort of. She applies for a role, but not the VP opportunity I'd suggested. Something "safer," she thought.

Fast forward to the interview. Trina walks in there and absolutely owns it. I'm talking jaws on the floor, minds blown. The hiring manager is so impressed, they're like, "Hold up. This woman isn't just good for the role she applied for. She's VP material."

Now, I wish I could say I played it cool when Trina told me this. But nah, I was doing a full-on victory dance. I didn't say "I told you so," but... well, I told you so.

So Trina goes back in for round two, this time gunning for that VP of Business Development role. And let me tell you, she owned that room like it was her personal stage at a TED Talk.

The result? They offered her the job on the spot. We're talking fully remote (hello, work-life balance!), a 45% pay bump, and equity that'll have her sipping margaritas on a beach when she's ready to retire.

The most compelling part is - Trina's happier than she's ever been. She's doing amazing work in her new role, setting an example for her daughter that would make any mom proud, and finally, finally reaping the rewards of all that dedication she's been cultivating for years.

Now, let me break this down for you, because there's a lesson here that you need to implanted in your mind:

- You are your own best advocate. Nobody - and I mean nobody - is going to promote you better than you can promote yourself.
- That voice in your head telling you you're not ready? It's a lie. Trina almost sold herself short, and look what happened when she didn't.
- Sometimes, you need someone to give you a push. Find that person who sees your potential and listen to them.
- Your skills are transferable. Trina went from individual sales to VP of Business Development. Don't let your current title limit your future.
- When you bet on yourself, the payoff can be huge. We're talking about life-changing money and opportunities here.

Trina's situation reminds me of a stat from a 2014 Hewlett Packard (HP) internal report, women generally apply for jobs only if they meet 100% of the qualifications, while men tend to apply when they meet about 60%. So, what's your next move? Are you going to stay within your comfort zone, or are you ready to break through and aim high like Trina?

Keep in mind the words of Marianne Williamson: "Playing small does not serve the world.

We've gone over a lot in this chapter. I want to drive this point home. There I was, fresh MBA in hand, leadership experience under my belt, and a history in recruiting and accounting. You'd think I'd be gunning for a corner office, right? Nope. I was in a new state and about to do something that would make most of my classmates scratch their heads.

I took an entry-level sales job.

Now, before you start wondering if I'd lost my marbles, let me tell you - I had a plan. And it involved a whole lot more than just cold calling and quota chasing.

I've always been a problem solver at heart. Give me a Rubik's cube of business challenges, and I'll twist and turn until everything clicks into place. So when I joined this company - a real heavy hitter in the industry - I wasn't just looking at the sales floor. I was eyeing the whole ecosystem, hunting for problems I could solve.

But let's be real for a second. This move? It was a financial gut punch. We're talking a nosedive in salary, responsibility, and comfort. To keep the lights on and maintain my lifestyle, I moonlighted as an adjunct accounting professor at a local career college. Talk about burning the candle at both ends!

You know that old saying, "Sometimes you have to take a step back to take a leap forward"? Well, I was living it. And let me tell you, it wasn't always pretty.

Sales was... well, it was a whole new world. In sales, you have to master the art of persuasion, read people like books, and bounce back from rejection like you're made of rubber. And when it comes to promoting yourself? You need to become your own biggest cheerleader without coming off as an egomaniac. It's a delicate dance, and I was just learning the steps.

But here is a confession- I couldn't let the company know I was out of my element. During my interview, I looked those interviewers straight in the eye and said, "I'll accept and commit to this role if offered, I'll audition if I need to but my goal is to get back into leadership as quickly as I can so that I can join you as a colleague" Bold? You bet. But that confidence, mixed with my experience, had them calling me with a job offer before I even left the parking lot.

Now, most people can sell anything - except themselves. It's like we're all walking around with these amazing products (ourselves) but we've misplaced the instruction manual. I was determined to crack that code.

So I dived in headfirst. I leveraged my network like it was going out of style. I devoured LinkedIn training sessions like they were the last slice of pizza at a party. I became a micro-learning machine, picking up new skills daily.

And you know what? This practice of constant learning and growth? It paid off big time. It helped me monetize my career because I became a versatile, adaptable asset. In a world where the only constant is change, being able to pivot and grow became my superpower. And let me tell you, employers eat that up like it's their favorite dessert.

When most people hear "monetizing your career," they immediately think of fat bonuses or landing that next big promotion. But let me tell you, that's just scratching the surface. It's like thinking the only way to get rich is by winning the lottery - you're missing out on all the real opportunities.

Many people struggle with identifying their unique strengths to start a side hustle, but my journey to financial freedom through portfolio careers and side hustles has taught me a valuable lesson: our most marketable skills are often hiding in plain sight. I've seen countless professionals overlook their most valuable assets: the skills and talents that come naturally to them.
In my experience, the key to unlocking your potential for lucrative

side hustles lies in recognizing and leveraging the abilities you may be taking for granted. This is why in this chapter, we'll explore how to identify and monetize these hidden gems, transforming your effortless abilities into profitable ventures.

Before we dive into the strategies, let's address a common pitfall that I've observed in many aspiring entrepreneurs: knowledge blindness. This phenomenon often stands between professionals and their potential for successful side hustles. Many of us become so accustomed to our skills that we fail to recognize their true value. We often think, "If it's easy for me, it must be easy for everyone." This couldn't be further from the truth.

By overcoming this knowledge blindness and learning to see our natural talents through a new lens, we can uncover opportunities for side hustles and portfolio careers that not only generate additional income but can potentially lead to complete financial freedom. Let's explore five powerful ways to uncover your monetizable skills and set you on the path to turning your hidden talents into thriving ventures.

Five Powerful Ways to Uncover Your Monetizable Skills:

Identify Your "Zone of Genius"
Your zone of genius is where your natural talents intersect with your passions. It's the sweet spot where work feels effortless and time flies by. To uncover this:
- List tasks you excel at without much effort
- Note activities that energize rather than drain you
- Reflect on moments when you've felt "in the flow"

Remember, what comes easily to you might be a struggle for others – and therein lies your opportunity.

Analyze Your Problem-Solving Skills

We all have unique ways of approaching challenges. Your problem-solving method could be the key to your next business venture. Consider:
- What issues do people frequently come to you for help with?
- How do you break down complex problems?
- What innovative solutions have you developed in your field?

Your approach to overcoming obstacles could be the foundation for a consulting business or a problem-solving framework that others would pay to learn.

Examine Your Daily Habits

Often, our most valuable skills are embedded in our daily routines. These habits, so ingrained that we barely notice them, can be goldmines of opportunity. Ask yourself:
- What productive activities do you do without thinking?
- Which organizational systems come naturally to you?
- How do you manage your time and energy efficiently?

These seemingly mundane habits could be the basis for productivity courses, time management apps, or organizational coaching services.

Leverage Your Communication Style

Your unique way of conveying information can be a powerful asset. Whether you're a natural storyteller, a data visualizer, or a master of simplifying complex concepts, your communication style can set you apart. Reflect on:
- How do you naturally explain ideas to others?
- What formats do you prefer when sharing information (visual, written, verbal)?
- Have you received compliments on your presentation or writing skills?

Your communication style could be the foundation for a successful speaking career, a writing business, or a unique approach to training and education.

Assess Your Emotional Intelligence
In today's interconnected world, emotional intelligence is more valuable than ever. Your ability to navigate interpersonal dynamics can be a highly marketable skill. Consider:
- How do you build and maintain relationships?
- Are you adept at resolving conflicts or mediating disputes?
- Can you easily read and respond to others' emotions?

These skills could be the basis for leadership coaching, team-building workshops, or conflict resolution services.

Turning Insight into Income
Once you've identified your natural talents, the next step is to package them into products or services that solve real problems for your target market. This might involve:
- Creating online courses or workshops
- Offering one-on-one coaching or consulting
- Developing digital products like eBook's or apps
- Building a personal brand around your unique expertise

Remember, the key is to start with what you already know and do well. Don't fall into the trap of thinking you need to acquire new skills before you can start monetizing your talents. Your existing abilities, properly positioned and marketed, are likely more than enough to launch a successful venture.

Monetizing your career is about playing the long game. It's about transforming yourself into a valuable asset that pays dividends over time. Think of it like this: You're not just an employee, you're a one-person corporation, and you're investing in your own stock.

It's learning new skills that make you irreplaceable. It's mastering the art of negotiation so you can advocate for yourself like a pro. It's taking your expertise and packaging it up with a bow, ready to sell to others as a course or eBook for those who need it. And sometimes, it's rolling up your sleeves and diving into projects that might not pay off immediately, but give you skills and visibility that'll compound over time. In essence, monetizing your career is about seeing the value in every experience, every connection, every challenge. It's about understanding that sometimes, the most valuable currency isn't in your paycheck - it's in your skillset, your network, and your reputation.

This requires a BIG mindset shift, I get it! I would share anything with you that I haven't personally done myself. Go back to the chapter,: "**Amplify Your Inner Confidence: Building a Confident Personal Brand**" and remind yourself of the value that you bring. Promote Your Damn Self: Because No One Else Will Do It For You.

Promote Your D@mn Self shows you how to see the value in every experience, connection, and challenge. It's about understanding that true career currency lies in your skillset, network, and reputation - not just your paycheck.

Don't wait for recognition - create it. Invest in yourself like you're the hottest stock on the market.

THINGS TO REMEMBER FROM THIS CHAPTER

Turning Opportunities into Success Stories

Your unique way of seeing the world is your greatest asset. Use it to create opportunities. Think about your "epiphany moment" – when did you realize your unique strength? Write it down and use it in your pitches.

Turning Free into Paid

Remember, every free opportunity is a potential gateway to paid work. After speaking events, offer a free consultation. On podcasts, mention a free resource on your website. In your book, include a link to a paid course.

Leverage Corporate Currency for Financial Wealth

Your corporate currency goes beyond salary—it's your skills, knowledge, network, and reputation. Every project, presentation, and process improvement is a chance to boost your value. Don't just work; invest in continuous learning, strategic networking, and showcasing your expertise. A $5,000 raise today could add up to $600,000 over your career. Are you fully leveraging your corporate currency?

Let's take action:

Write a LinkedIn post using the above template to share a recent achievement or offer.

Every "no" brings you closer to a "yes." Every free opportunity is a stepping stone to paid work. Every connection can lead to a life-changing opportunity. You've got what it takes to create opportunities for yourself—now go out there and shine!

YOUR NOTES:

Take a moment to reflect

YOUR NOTES:

Take a moment to reflect

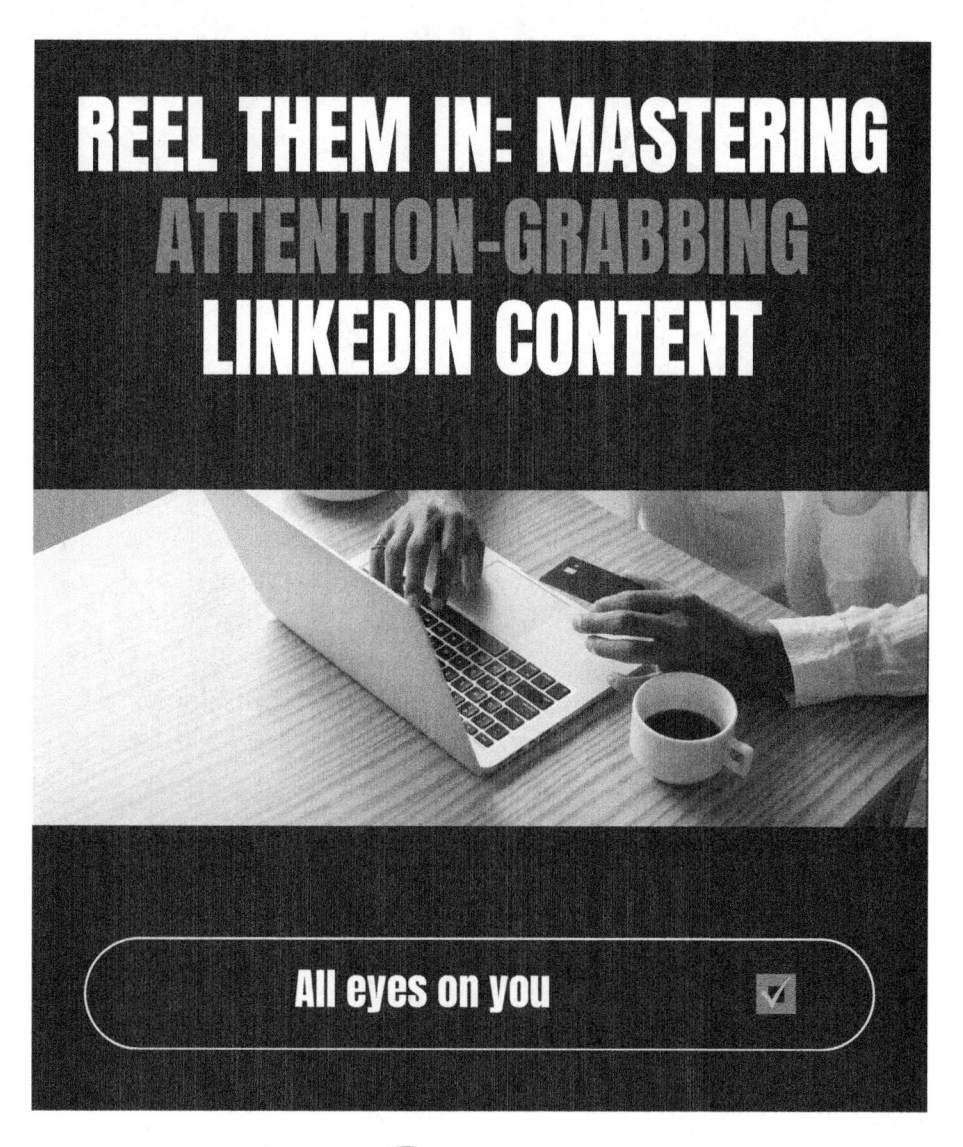

REEL THEM IN: MASTERING ATTENTION-GRABBING LINKEDIN CONTENT

All eyes on you

What you will learn

Engineer your LinkedIn success with precision-crafted content templates. Discover how to leverage these powerful tools to create a steady stream of engaging posts that attract opportunities and accelerate your professional growth.

REEL THEM IN: MASTERING ATTENTION-GRABBING

I see that you are still with me. That is a good sign. If you've made it this far, thank you for your dedication and trust in this journey. Your commitment to growing your personal brand is commendable, and I'm grateful you've chosen to invest your time in these pages. We're now about to take a journey that'll transform you from a content novice to a LinkedIn legend. This isn't just about creating content; it's about crafting digital magic that stops scrolling thumbs in their tracks and sets minds on fire.

Your content isn't just competing with other professionals; it's up against cat videos, TikTok dances, and the entire attention economy.

According to a study by Microsoft, the average human attention span has dropped to eight seconds. How do you capture attention in a world where the average human attention span has dwindled to a mere 8 seconds—just two seconds less than that of a goldfish? So, we've got to make every second count. This challenge becomes even more daunting when you consider the following statistics:

- People check their phones an astounding 96 times a day—that's once every 10 minutes.
- The average person spends 3 hours and 15 minutes on their phone daily.
- 70% of social media time is spent on mobile devices.
- LinkedIn boasts over 1 billion plus members, with 57% accessing it via mobile devices.

The LinkedIn Conundrum

When I first started posting on LinkedIn, I was like many others—caught in the cycle of generic congratulatory notes and work anniversary wishes. I followed the unwritten "rules" of the platform, mimicking what I saw others do. After all, isn't LinkedIn the place to celebrate work-related things isn't that what LinkedIn is primarily known for?

In a world where:
- 70% of people check their phones within 5 minutes of receiving a notification
- Mobile devices account for 70% of digital media time
- "Near me" or "close by" type searches grew by more than 900% over two years

The key to standing out lies in understanding these mobile behaviors and crafting content that resonates with on-the-go professionals. It's about creating moments that make busy executives pause mid-scroll, compelling them to engage with your ideas even as notifications flood their screens.

This chapter will guide you through the process of transforming your LinkedIn presence from just another tile in the endless scroll to a powerful magnet for opportunities. We'll explore strategies to leverage the mobile-first mindset, optimize your content for quick consumption, and create the kind of value that keeps your audience coming back for more—all while staying true to your unique brand voice.

Get ready to turn those seven seconds of attention into meaningful connections, thought leadership, and career-advancing opportunities. Welcome to the art of scroll-stopping content creation.

The Seven-Second Challenge

Before we dive into the strategies, let's consider this startling statistic: according to a 2015 study by Microsoft, the average human attention span has dropped to eight seconds, down from twelve seconds in 2000. More recent studies suggest it might be even lower now, around seven seconds.

This means that when someone is scrolling through their LinkedIn feed, you have less time than it takes to tie a shoelace to grab their attention. It's a daunting challenge, but one that can be overcome with the right approach.

You're scrolling through LinkedIn, mindlessly flicking past post after post. Suddenly, something catches your eye. Your thumb freezes. Your eyes widen. You've just encountered scroll-stopping content. That, my friend, is what we're aiming for.

The secret weapon? It's not about dazzle and flash. It's about diving deep into the human psyche. We're creatures of narrative, emotion, and connection. That's your golden key to forging instant bonds.

Remember Trina? Her experience isn't just a feel-good story—it's a roadmap to success. She transformed from a wallflower plagued by self-doubt into a powerhouse of self-promotion, catapulting from the trenches to the executive suite.

Secret #1: The Art of Content Observation

The first step in creating scroll-stopping content is understanding what makes **YOU** stop scrolling. This self-reflection is crucial because it helps you identify the elements that captivate your own attention, which can then be applied to your content strategy.Think about the last piece of content that made you stop scrolling. According to LinkedIn, posts with images get 2x higher engagement. Videos? They get 5x more engagement than any other type of content on the platform. But here's the kicker: Only 1% of LinkedIn users share content regularly. That's your opportunity right there.

What was it about that post that grabbed you? Was it the headline? The image? The opening line? Analyze it, learn from it, and apply those lessons to your own content.

EXERCISE: THE LINKEDIN FEED ANALYSIS

Set aside 20-30 minutes and grab a notebook (digital or physical). Now, start scrolling through your LinkedIn feed with a critical eye. For each post you encounter, ask yourself:

- Does this make me want to keep scrolling, or does it make me stop?
- If I want to scroll past, why? Is it too long? Uninteresting? Poorly formatted?
- If it makes me stop, what exactly caught my eye? Was it the opening line? An image? A surprising statistic?
- How does the post make me feel? Intrigued? Inspired? Skeptical?
- What's the engagement like? Are there thoughtful comments or just generic responses?

This exercise isn't just about identifying what you like—it's about understanding the psychology behind engaging content. You're training your eye to spot the elements that make a post stand out in a sea of information.

Case Study: The Power of Authenticity

Let me share a personal anecdote. Early in my LinkedIn journey, I came across a post that stopped me mid-scroll. It wasn't from a CEO or a famous influencer—it was from a mid-level manager sharing a vulnerable moment of failure and the lessons learned from it. The post had thousands of engagements, with comments full of support and shared experiences.

This post taught me a valuable lesson: authenticity and vulnerability can be more powerful than polished corporate speech. It inspired me to share my own stories of challenges and growth, which led to a significant increase in my engagement rates.

Viral content:

You can't predict what will go viral. But you can increase your chances. How? By tapping into universal human experiences. Talk about fear, ambition, failure, success, love, hate. These are the threads that connect us all.

Let me tell you about Rosie. Rosie was a brilliant customer success manager, head down, creating magic behind the scenes. She was the last person you'd expect to become a "content creator." In fact, when I first suggested she share her insights on LinkedIn, she looked at me like I'd grown a second head.

"I'm not trying to be an influencer," she said, rolling her eyes. "I just want to do my job." But here's the thing about Rosie- she had a story that needed to be told. As a woman in tech, she'd encountered more hurdles than a track star at the Olympics. She'd broken barriers, shattered stereotypes, and paved the way for others. And she'd done it all while battling imposter syndrome that would've crippled a lesser person.

One day, after a particularly grueling project, I convinced Rosie to share her experience on LinkedIn. Just one post, I promised. No hashtags, no fancy graphics, just her raw, honest story.

That single post exploded. It racked up thousands of views, and hundreds of comments, and sparked conversations across the industry. Rosie's inbox was flooded with messages from young women inspired by her journey, from managers wanting to create more inclusive teams, to recruiters offering her dream jobs.

At that moment, Rosie realized something profound: She wasn't just a customer success manager. She was a voice. A beacon. A change-maker.

And that, my friend, is the power of content. It's not about becoming an influencer or chasing likes. It's about sharing your unique perspective, your hard-earned wisdom, your human experience. Because somewhere out there, someone needs to hear exactly what you have to say.

Remember that your story, your insights, your experiences - they matter. They have the power to inspire, to educate, to transform. You're not just creating content. You're creating change. One post at a time. Here's a tip that'll set you apart: Create content that creates content. Ask questions that compel your audience to share their own stories in the comments. That's not just engagement; that's content multiplication.

Seth Godin emphasizes storytelling in marketing over products. Your content is your story. Don't worry if you're not a natural storyteller. Effective content storytelling is about authentically sharing experiences and value that resonate with your audience.

Secret #2: Know Your Audience (and Yourself)

Creating content that resonates isn't just about understanding what works on LinkedIn—it's about understanding who you're talking to and why they should care.

The Target Audience Blueprint

Before you write a single word, ask yourself:

- Who am I trying to reach? (e.g., hiring managers, potential clients, industry peers)
- What problems do they face that I can help solve?
- How can I add value to their professional lives?

But here's the twist: while you're considering your audience, don't lose sight of yourself. The most compelling content comes from a place of genuine interest and expertise.

The "Letter to Self" Technique

One of the most effective techniques I've developed is what I call the "Letter to Self" method. Here's how it works:

1. Imagine you're writing to your younger self or to someone you deeply care about.
2. Start your draft with "Dear [Name],"
3. Write your post as if you're giving advice or sharing insights with this person.
4. End with "Your future self,"
5. When you're ready to post, remove the salutation and sign-off, but keep the core content.

I believe that consistent, value-packed content is the single most powerful tool for career advancement in the digital age. It's not just about what you know; it's about how effectively you share it. Here's a secret that'll blow your mind: The best content often comes from your struggles, not your successes. That project you messed up? The presentation that flopped? That's gold. People connect with vulnerability, with real human experiences.

This technique accomplishes two things: it makes your writing more personal and relatable, and it taps into the genuine desire to help that often produces the most valuable content.

What's the biggest challenge you're facing right now in your career? That's not just a problem; it's a content opportunity.

Share your journey, your attempts to overcome it. Watch how people rally around you.

Secret #3: The L.E.A.D Framework

Now that you understand your audience and have tapped into your authentic voice, it's time to structure your content for maximum impact. The Recipe for Scroll-Stopping Content

L- Lead and Hook 'em fast: You've got 3 seconds to grab attention. Make them count.

E- Elaborate: Tell a story: Humans are wired for narratives. Give them one.

A- Articulate the message: Don't just entertain; educate. What's the takeaway? What wisdom are you imparting? This is where you transition from storyteller to mentor.

D- Drive Action: You've hooked them, you've moved them, you've taught them. Now, what do you want them to do? Comment? Share? Connect? (This is referred to as a call to action (CTA))

The 'D' in L.E.A.D. isn't just about driving action in your audience. It's a reminder that you're in the driver's seat. You're not just creating content; you're leading a conversation, steering minds, and shaping perspectives.

Remember, in the content game, you're not just a player; you're the damn captain. The L.E.A.D. framework is your reminder that with every post, you have the power to Lead, to Elaborate, to Articulate, and to Drive.

So the next time you're staring at that blank LinkedIn post, feeling the cursor mock you with its incessant blinking, remember: You're not just writing a post. You're leading a movement. One scroll-stopping post at a time.

Here is an example of how the L.E.A.D. framework comes together:

The best leaders talk the least.' This counterintuitive advice from today's seminar stopped me in my tracks.

For years, I thought leadership meant having all the answers. I'd dominate meetings, rarely pausing for input. The result? A disengaged team and missed opportunities.

Today, I learned the power of strategic silence. By talking less

Here is how to build a post by breaking the L.E.A.D. framework down piece by piece.

Lead with a Hook: You have seven seconds, remember? Your opening line (often called a hook), needs to be sharp, surprising, or intriguing enough to make someone pause their scrolling.

Example: "I once turned down a $100,000 job offer. It was the best career move I ever made."

Elaborate with a Story: Once you've got their attention, you need to keep it. This is where storytelling comes in. Share an anecdote, pose a thought-provoking question, or present a startling fact.

Articulate the Lesson: What's the takeaway? Every post should provide value and/ or lessons, whether it's a new perspective, a practical tip, or an inspiring idea.

Drive Action: End with a call to action. Invite comments, ask for opinions, or encourage sharing of similar experiences. This turns your post from a monologue into a conversation.

Putting It All Together: A Case Study

Let's look at how this framework can transform a typical LinkedIn post:

Before (Generic Post):

Just finished an amazing leadership seminar! Learned so much about effective communication and team building. #Leadership #ProfessionalDevelopment

After (Using L.E.A.D. Framework):

The best leaders talk the least.' This counterintuitive advice from today's seminar stopped me in my tracks.

For years, I thought leadership meant having all the answers. I'd dominate meetings, rarely pausing for input. The result? A disengaged team and missed opportunities.

Today, I learned the power of strategic silence. By talking less and listening more, leaders create space for diverse ideas and foster true collaboration.

What's one leadership myth you've had to unlearn? Share below—let's build a resource of real leadership insights together.

LinkedIn has evolved beyond just text. Consider using a mix of:
- Text posts
- Carousel posts
- Videos (short and long)
- Articles
- Polls
- Live streams
- Documents

The key? Diversify and find what resonates with you and your audience. Variety keeps engagement high.

Here's a groundbreaking tip that no one's talking about:

The Content Multiplication Method: Turning One Idea into 20

- **Self-interview:** Ask yourself questions about your expertise. Each answer becomes a post.
- **Comment mining:** Address recurring questions from popular industry posts.
- **Retrospective wisdom:** Share insights you wish you'd known earlier in your career.
- **Leverage novelty bias:** Incorporate fresh perspectives to captivate your audience.

This approach taps into the brain's natural attraction to new information, making your content more engaging and memorable.

The human brain's inherent fascination with novelty, known as the "novelty bias," is a powerful psychological phenomenon that can be leveraged in various aspects of life and work. This bias explains why we're naturally drawn to new experiences, ideas, and information, as our brains release dopamine in response to novelty. By incorporating fresh perspectives, unique angles, or surprising twists into your work or communication, you can captivate your audience's attention and make your message more memorable and impactful.

The Resilience Factor

Creating content that consistently engages isn't easy. There will be posts that fall flat, ideas that don't resonate, and days when the inspiration just isn't there. This is where resilience comes in.

Remember:

- Every "failed" post is a data point, not a defeat.
- Consistency begets perfection. It's better to post regularly and improve over time than to wait for the "perfect" post.

- Engage with others genuinely. The connections you build will support you through the ups and downs.

By now, you've learned several key strategies: content analysis, authentic voice development, effective post structuring, and resilience-building for LinkedIn success. However, this knowledge is only valuable when put into action consistently.

Success on LinkedIn doesn't happen overnight - it requires persistent effort and continuous learning.

As you begin applying these new concepts, you may encounter questions or obstacles. Don't hesitate to seek support and guidance. The Promote Your D@mn Self community on LinkedIn is an excellent resource for professionals like you. We're here to support your journey, answer your questions, and help you transform those ideas from mere thoughts into impactful content that resonates with your network.

Your Challenge:

1. Conduct your LinkedIn feed analysis today.
2. Write your first post using the L.E.A.D. framework.
3. Commit to posting at least twice a week for the next month.
4. Engage with at least 5 other posts daily.

Remember, you have the power to turn a 8-second attention span into a lasting impression. Your unique experiences, insights, and voice are valuable. It's time to stop scrolling and start sharing.

If you are still need content and posting guidance, sign up for the [Promote Your D@mn Self 18day LinkedIn Visibility Challenge](#)

where you will get the exact recommendations of what to post, how to grow your following, secrets and tricks that NO ONE is talking about, gaining brand authority, and live coaching on how to use these tips to grow your professional career, thought leadership, or business. Sign up by following this link.

https://shantel-love-llc.ck.page/products/18-day-linked-in-visibility-challenge

We've unlocked the secrets of scroll-stopping content, dived deep into the psychology of engagement, and learned how to turn our experiences into digital value.

But here's the thing - all the tips, tricks, and techniques in the world don't mean anything if you don't take action. Knowledge without application is about as useful as a screen door on a submarine. So here's my challenge to you: Take one idea from this chapter - just one - and put it into action today. Not tomorrow, not next week, today. Create that post you've been mulling over. Share that story you've been hesitant to tell. Start that conversation you've been yearning to have.

Remember, you're not just creating content. You're creating connections. You're creating opportunities. You're creating your future.

In the words of the great Maya Angelou, "There is no greater agony than bearing an untold story inside you." So let it out. Let your voice be heard. Let your content be the pebble that starts a ripple of change across your industry.

Because here's the brutal truth: In today's digital age, if you're not visible, you're invisible. Your brilliance, your expertise, your unique perspective - they mean nothing if they're locked away in the vault of your mind.

THINGS TO REMEMBER FROM THIS CHAPTER

1. Mobile-first content is crucial: With 70% of social media time spent on mobile devices, creating content that resonates with on-the-go professionals is key.

2. You have 8 seconds to capture attention: The average human attention span has decreased to about 8 seconds, making it essential to create scroll-stopping content.

3. Authenticity and vulnerability are powerful: Sharing genuine experiences and challenges can lead to higher engagement than polished corporate content.

4. Use the L.E.A.D. framework: Lead with a Hook, Elaborate with a Story, Articulate the Lesson, and Drive Action to structure impactful posts.

5. Consistency and resilience are vital: Regular posting and learning from both successes and failures are crucial for long-term success on LinkedIn.

LET'S TAKE ACTION

Conduct a LinkedIn feed analysis today. Spend 20-30 minutes scrolling through your feed, critically examining posts that make you stop or want to keep scrolling. Take notes on what catches your attention, what doesn't, and why. Use these insights to inform your own content creation strategy.

YOUR NOTES:

Take a moment to reflect

YOUR NOTES:

Take a moment to reflect

PERSONAL BRAND BUILDING AS A JOB SEEKER

Build during your job search ☑

What you will learn

The job seeker's ultimate LinkedIn strategy: Stand out in a sea of applicants. Master the art of personal branding that turns your profile into a compelling career narrative, making recruiters reach for the phone.

PERSONAL BRAND BUILDING AS A JOB SEEKER

It was 2:37 AM, and Jerlene was staring at her laptop screen, the harsh blue light illuminating her tired face. She'd just applied to her 127th job in three months. Yes, she was counting. Each application felt like shouting into the Bermuda triangle, hoping someone, anyone, would hear her.

"There has to be a better way," she muttered, scrolling mindlessly through LinkedIn.

That's when she saw it. A post from an old colleague, Moe:

"Excited to announce I've landed my dream job at Tesla! Thanks to everyone who supported me on this journey. #NewBeginnings #PersonalBrand"

Jerlene's first reaction was a mix of jealousy and frustration. But as she dug deeper into Moe's profile, something clicked. His LinkedIn wasn't just a digital resume; it was a showcase of his expertise, his passion, his... brand.

And that's when the epiphany hit her like a bucket of ice water and she hired me as her coach.

She'd been playing the job search game all wrong. In a world where 75% of recruiters use LinkedIn to vet candidates before hiring, and 40% of employers use social media to screen applicants, Sarah realized she'd been invisible. Just another faceless resume amongst of thousands.

But what if she could stand out? What if she could make recruiters come to her?

Let's pause here for a moment. Does this sound familiar? Have you felt that late-night frustration, wondering if your applications are disappearing into a black hole? You're not alone. In fact, the average job opening receives 250 resumes, but only 2% of applicants actually get an interview.

Now, ask yourself:

1. What unique value do I bring that isn't reflected in my current LinkedIn profile?
2. If I were a recruiter looking at my profile, would I be intrigued or just see another generic candidate?
3. What's holding me back from putting myself out there more boldly?

Jerlene spent the next few weeks transforming her LinkedIn presence. She started sharing insights from her field, commenting thoughtfully on industry leaders' posts, and even published a few articles showcasing her expertise.

It wasn't easy. Every time she hit "post," a voice in her head whispered, "Who do you think you are?" But she pushed through, reminding herself that 91% of executives see LinkedIn as their first choice for professionally relevant content.

Slowly but surely, things started to change. Her network grew. Recruiters started reaching out to her. And three months later, she landed a job that was better than anything she'd applied for.

But here's the thing: the job found her. A recruiter came across one of her articles and reached out directly. Jerlene had become the diamond in a pile of rocks.

Now, I know what you're thinking. "That's great for Jerlene, but my situation is different." Maybe you're worried about seeming desperate, or you're not sure how to balance job seeking with building a side hustle. Perhaps you're thinking, "I'm not an expert. Who would want to hear what I have to say?"

These are all valid concerns. But consider this: in a job market where 85% of jobs are filled through networking, can you afford not to build your personal brand?

So, let me ask you:

1. What's the story you want to tell about your professional journey?
2. If you could be known for one thing in your industry, what would it be?
3. What's the worst that could happen if you start sharing your insights and experiences?

Your expertise is a story of growth. Each challenge overcome and lesson learned shapes your unique professional narrative. In today's marketplace, this personal journey isn't just a footnote—it's your standout feature. Embrace and showcase it to distinguish yourself from the crowd.

Meet Alex, a marketing professional who'd been job hunting for 8 months. Every rejection felt like a punch to the gut. "I was at my lowest point," Alex told me. "I'd applied to over 200 jobs and hadn't landed a single interview. I was ready to give up."
That's when Alex decided to try something different. Instead of

sending out more resumes, they committed to sharing one marketing insight on LinkedIn every day for 30 days. "It was terrifying at first," Alex admitted. "I felt like an imposter. But I kept going."

By day 15, something shifted. Alex's posts started gaining traction. By day 30, a recruiter reached out. Two weeks later, Alex had three job offers on the table. Guess what? None of these were jobs Alex had applied for. They came to Alex.

"It wasn't just about the job offers," Alex reflected. "The process of sharing my knowledge daily rebuilt my confidence. I remembered why I loved marketing in the first place."

Job seeking can be a mental battlefield. Rejection after rejection can wear down even the toughest minds. But here's a perspective shift that can change everything: think of job seeking not as begging for opportunities, but as auditioning employers for the privilege of having you on their team.

This mindset shift is powerful because it puts you back in control. You're not a desperate applicant; you're a valuable asset evaluating potential partnerships. This subtle change can dramatically boost your confidence and how you present yourself online.

Let's talk about staying positive:
- **Celebrate small wins:** Did you learn a new skill today? Make a new connection? Share it on LinkedIn. Each post is a victory, regardless of the immediate outcome.
- **Practice gratitude:** Start each day by posting one thing you're grateful for in your professional life. This trains your brain to focus on the positive.

- **Visualize success:** Before you write a post, imagine it resonating with your dream employer. This positive visualization can improve your writing and your mood.
- **Embrace rejection as redirection:** When you don't get a job, post about what you learned from the experience. This reframes rejection as growth.

Job seekers, I see you. I know the frustration—the endless applications, the silence, the self-doubt. I've been there. The job market feels like a maze of dead ends and false starts. But you're still here, still fighting. That resilience? It's your power.

Now, let's channel that determination into a LinkedIn strategy that stands out. Transform your profile from a digital resume into a magnet for opportunity. Imagine employers seeking you out.
It's possible. I've seen it happen, and I believe it can happen for you.

We'll dive deep into LinkedIn techniques that work, crafting a personal brand so compelling, employers can't look away. It won't be easy—it might push you out of your comfort zone—but remember, every successful job seeker once stood where you are now. The difference? They took the next step.

First things first, let's talk about attracting recruiters. Here's the deal:

1. **Engage, engage, engage:** Don't just lurk in the shadows. Comment on posts from industry leaders, share insights, and use relevant hashtags. Recruiters are like rottweilers sniffing out active participants.

2. **Publish articles:** Yeah, I know it sounds like a pain, but trust me. Writing about industry trends or sharing your expertise makes you look like a thought leader. Recruiters eat that stuff up.

3. **Be Specific In Your Headline:** Instead of "Marketing Professional," try "Digital Marketing Specialist | SEO Wizard | Content Strategy Guru." It's like catnip for recruiters.

4. **Boolean Search Optimization:** Recruiters use Boolean searches to find candidates. Make sure your profile is rich with keywords relevant to her industry.

5. **SEO-Friendly Content:** Treat your LinkedIn profile like a personal website, optimizing your headline, summary, and experience sections with industry-specific keywords. Your summary should be a compelling narrative that highlights your achievements and value proposition.

6. **Engaging Visual Content:** Consider posting short videos where you share industry tips and insights. These videos not only showcased your expertise but also your personality and communication skills.

7. **Monthly Posting Series:** To really stand out, launch a monthly posting series on LinkedIn where you share industry trends, case studies, and practical tips. This can position you as a thought leader and keep you top-of-mind with her network.

As you reflect on the above suggestions, I want to share new perspective for job seekers:

By actively engaging on LinkedIn, you position yourself as a thought leader, gain visibility with industry professionals, and open doors to opportunities that go beyond the traditional job search. It's not just about finding a job—it's about creating a professional presence that attracts the right opportunities to you.

Here's an actionable 5-day LinkedIn challenge for job seekers:

Day 1: Reveal a significant career challenge you've conquered. Embrace vulnerability.
Day 2: Spotlight an emerging trend in your industry. Prove you're ahead of the curve.
Day 3: Showcase a skill you're honing. Exemplify continuous growth.
Day 4: Share a book or podcast that's shaped your professional journey. Inspire with curiosity.
Day 5: Reflect on the week. What have you learned? How have you evolved?

Consistency is crucial. Focus on showing up daily, not on going viral. When networking, shift from asking for jobs to seeking advice. People enjoy being helpful, and this lessens the pressure on them while creating more opportunities for you. Reach out to admired professionals for their insights.

Template : Reaching Out To Professionals For Advice

Subject: Seeking your valuable insights on [specific area/industry]

Hi [Name],

I hope this message finds you well. My name is [Your Name], and I've been following your work in [their field/industry] with great admiration. Your recent [post/article/achievement] on [specific topic] particularly resonated with me.

I'm currently navigating my career in [your field], and I'm eager to learn from experienced professionals like yourself. I would be incredibly grateful if you could spare 15-20 minutes for a brief call or coffee chat (virtual or in-person) to share your insights on [1-2 specific questions or areas you'd like advice on].

I'm particularly interested in hearing your thoughts on:
- *[Specific question or area of interest]*
- *[Another specific question or area of interest]*

I understand you're busy, and I appreciate any time you can offer. Your perspective would be invaluable to me as I work to grow in this field.

Thank you for considering my request. I look forward to the possibility of connecting with you.

Best regards,
[Your Name]

Remember to personalize this template based on the individual you're reaching out to and your specific situation.

Here are some key points to keep in mind when using this approach:
1. **Be specific:** Mention something recent they've done or posted to show you've done your homework.
2. **Keep it brief:** Respect their time by being concise.
3. **Offer options:** Suggest a short call or coffee chat, and be open to either virtual or in-person meetings.
4. **Ask targeted questions:** Have 1-2 specific areas you want advice on, rather than asking for general career help.
5. **Show appreciation:** Acknowledge their busy schedule and express genuine gratitude for any time they can offer.
6. **Follow up:** If they agree to meet, send a thank-you note afterward summarizing what you learned and how you plan to apply their advice.

This approach positions you as a proactive learner rather than a job seeker, which can lead to more meaningful connections and potentially open doors to opportunities you hadn't considered.

Imposter syndrome: the silent killer of potential. Let's rip off the band-aid - if you feel like a fraud, you're not alone. A staggering 70% of professionals wrestle with imposter syndrome.
The most accomplished individuals aren't immune to imposter syndrome. They're masters at not letting it cement them. So embrace that uncertainty and use it as fuel. Post that content. Share your ideas. Step into the spotlight. Your voice matters.

Here's a radical idea: bare your scars. A candid account of your failures will resonate more than a thousand polished success stories. It's not just relatable - it's powerful. It shows grit, resilience, and an unquenchable thirst for growth.

> **NOW, ONTO BUILDING THAT PERSONAL BRAND WHILE JOB HUNTING.**

1. **Tell your story:** Use your "About" section to craft a compelling narrative. Talk about your journey, your passions, and where you want to go. It's not just a resume – it's your origin story.

Example "About" section:
From coding bootcamp graduate to lead developer at a Fortune 500 company, my journey has been anything but conventional. I'm passionate about using technology to solve real-world problems, whether it's streamlining healthcare systems or making education more accessible.

My superpower? Translating complex tech jargon into language anyone can understand. I believe that great software isn't just about clean code—it's about empowering users.

When I'm not knee-deep in code, you'll find me mentoring

aspiring developers or tinkering with my latest IoT project. My goal? To lead a tech team that creates products that genuinely improve lives.

Let's connect if you're interested in tech that makes a difference, or if you just want to geek out about the latest JavaScript framework!"

2. **Showcase your work:** Use LinkedIn's features to highlight projects, publications, or volunteer work. It's like your own little museum of awesomeness.

Example of how to use LinkedIn's features:
- **Projects section:** "AI-Powered Healthcare Chatbot" Description: Led a team of 5 to develop an AI chatbot that reduced patient wait times by 30%. Used Python, TensorFlow, and AWS.

- **Publications:** "The Future of EdTech: 5 Trends to Watch" Link to your Medium article or industry blog post.

- **Volunteer Experience:** "Code for America - Chapter Lead" Description: Organize monthly hackathons to build tech solutions for local non-profits.

3. **Video content:** I know, I know, you're not a TikTok star. But short video updates or insights can really make you stand out. Just keep it professional – save the dance challenges for another platform.

Example video script:
Hey LinkedIn! Quick tech tip of the week: Ever struggle with (60 seconds):

merge conflicts in Git? Here's a simple trick I use...

[Demonstrate the tip]

This has saved me hours of headaches. Try it out and let me know if it helps you too! What's your favorite Git trick? Drop it in the comments below.

And if you found this helpful, follow me for more weekly tech tips. See you next time!"

4. **Consistency is key:** Post regularly, but don't spam. Aim for 3-5 times a week. It's like dating – you want to be present, not desperate.

Template : Weekly Posting Schedule

Monday: Share an industry article with your thoughts
Just read this fascinating piece on quantum computing. Here's what it could mean for cybersecurity... [Your insights]"

Wednesday: Quick tip or trick related to your field
💡 Pro tip: Use this keyboard shortcut to boost your productivity in Excel... [Explain the tip]

Friday: Reflection on your week or a challenge you overcame
This week, I tackled my biggest code refactoring project yet. Here's what I learned... [Share lessons]

Remember, the key is to provide value to your network while

showcasing your expertise. Each post should either inform, educate, or inspire your connections. And don't forget to engage with others' content too - commenting thoughtfully on posts in your field can be just as powerful as creating your own content.

Promoting your side hustle without scaring off recruiters:

Now, here's where it gets tricky - promoting your side hustle without scaring off recruiters. I am a former recruiter and I have had a side hustle spanning two decades. That said, I've been around the block a few times, and let me tell you, navigating the whole "side hustle while job hunting" thing can be trickier than a game of Jenga after a few margaritas. But don't worry, I've got your back.

So, you've got this amazing side hustle, right? And you're wanting to talk about it on your LinkedIn profile. However, you don't want potential employers thinking you're not 100% committed to your day job. It's like trying to convince your partner you're totally focused on your relationship while also swiping on Tinder. Tricky business, my friend.

Here's how to do it:

Frame it as professional development:

Don't just mention that you're expanding your skills - get specific. Are you learning about digital marketing through your Etsy shop? Honing your project management skills by organizing local events? Spell it out. Show them how your side hustle is making you a better catch for their company.

Keep it relevant:

Absolutely. If your side hustle aligns with your career, it's like match matching and you become the ideal match. But sometimes our passions don't line up neatly. If you're a software engineer by day and a yoga instructor by night, focus on those transferable skills. Talk about how teaching yoga has improved your communication skills or how managing your class schedule has sharpened your time management game. It's all about spinning that story.

Use the Featured section:

The Featured section is like that fancy guest bathroom you only use for company - it's where you put the good stuff. But here's a pro tip: create a visually appealing graphic or infographic about your side business to feature. It's eye-catching and shows you've got some design expertise (or at least know how to use Canva).

Be strategic with your connections:

Yes, yes, and yes. But let's take it up a notch. Create LinkedIn lists to organize your connections. This way, you can tailor your content sharing to different groups. Share your latest corporate accomplishments with your professional contacts, and your side hustle wins with your entrepreneurial circle. It's like having multiple personalities, but in a totally socially acceptable way.

At the end of the day, it's all about balance. You want to come across as passionate and driven, not scattered and uncommitted. It's like trying to eat a salad and a burger at the same time - tricky, but doable with the right approach.

You're not alone in this juggling act. Tons of people are out there hustling on the side while climbing the corporate ladder. The key is to own your story and show how your diverse experiences make you a unique and valuable asset.

Now, let's talk tools because in 2024, if you're not using AI, you're bringing a knife to a gunfight:

TEAL: This is a game-changer. It'll help you tailor your resume for each job application in minutes. It's like having a personal assistant doing all the grunt work.

Jasper.ai: Great for helping you craft compelling LinkedIn posts or articles. Just don't let it write everything – add your personal touch.

Dripify: This tool automates your LinkedIn outreach. Use it wisely – you don't want to come off as a spam-bot.

Photor.ai: For creating eye-catching visuals for your posts. Because let's face it, we're all attracted to eye-catching things.

Remember, in this job market, you've got to be the diamond in a pile of rocks. Don't be afraid to Promote Your D@mn Self. Share your failures along with your successes. Be human. Be authentic.

Your LinkedIn profile should be working harder than you are. Make it your own personal hype person, your 24/7 networking event, and your digital portfolio all rolled into one.

And here's a pro tip: Don't just connect with recruiters – engage with them. Comment on their posts, share their content. Make them remember you.

It's like planting seeds – you never know which one will grow into your dream job. Lastly, remember that building a personal brand is a marathon, not a sprint. It's okay to pivot, to experiment, to find your voice. The key is to keep moving forward, keep learning, and keep putting yourself out there.

Now go forth and conquer that LinkedIn game. You've got this, friend. And if all else fails, there's always goat yoga as a career option. (Kidding. Unless...?)

THINGS TO REMEMBER FROM THIS CHAPTER

- A strong LinkedIn presence is crucial in today's job market, with 75% of recruiters using it to vet candidates.

- Actively engaging on LinkedIn through comments, posts, and articles can make you stand out to recruiters.

- Consistency in posting (3-5 times a week) and content creation (like monthly series) helps maintain visibility.

- Utilize AI tools like TEAL, Jasper.ai, and Dripify to optimize your LinkedIn strategy and job search efforts.

LET'S TAKE ACTION:

Start engaging with industry-relevant content by commenting on at least 5 posts today. This will kickstart your visibility and personal branding efforts on the platform. Don't for get to visit the Promote Your D@mn Self community to engage there.

YOUR NOTES:

Take a moment to reflect

YOUR NOTES:

Take a moment to reflect

THE A.N.S.W.E.R. IS WITHIN YOU

Your Journey is just beginning ✓

What you will learn

Your Promote Your D@mn Self legacy starts now: Integrating key lessons for unstoppable career momentum. Learn how to weave together all the strategies you've discovered, creating a personal brand that opens doors you never knew existed.

THE A.N.S.W.E.R. IS WITHIN YOU

We've been through a lot together, haven't we? Remember when you first picked up this book? Perhaps you felt lost in the noise of personal branding, struggling to stand out in your field. That fear of being judged, of failure, might have held you back. But now? You're armed with knowledge that most professionals would give anything to possess.

And if you're sitting there thinking, "Damn, I need more help!"

I've got your back. You can find me at www.linkedin.com/in/shantellove or hit me up at info@shantellove.com for some extra coaching. And for those ready to really level up, check out the **Promote Your D@mn Self 18-day LinkedIn visibility challenge** at https://shantel-love-llc.ck.page/products/18-day-linked-in-visibility-challenge.

You've learned to shed your "liedentity" and embrace your authentic self. You learned how to avoid the **3 personal branding mistakes that nearly cost me my six-figure career**. My experience serves as a stark reminder of how easily one can stumble, yet also demonstrates the incredible power of a well-cultivated personal brand.

- **Mental Wealth:** The Foundation, we began with Mental Wealth, the cornerstone of personal branding that's all too often

overlooked. This isn't just about knowledge; it's about mindset, self-awareness, and emotional intelligence. By neglecting this crucial aspect, we risk building our professional image on shaky ground. Remember, your internal dialogue shapes your external presence.
- **Social Wealth:** The Amplifier Next, we explored Social Wealth, a factor that proved pivotal in empowering my journey to mentor, coach, and learn from those that I've connected with. In our hyper-connected world, your network truly is your net worth. But it goes beyond mere connections—it's about meaningful relationships and strategic interactions. LinkedIn, far from being just a job board, is a powerful platform for cultivating this wealth. Neglect this, and you're leaving an enormous opportunity on the table.
- **Financial Wealth:** The Culmination Finally, we addressed Financial Wealth—the art of monetizing your expertise and reputation. This is where your personal brand transforms from a concept into tangible economic value. It's not just about being known; it's about being known for something valuable. This pillar empowers you to "Promote Your D@mn Self" instead of waiting for others to recognize your worth.

My near-downfall and subsequent recovery underscore a crucial truth: your personal brand can be your lifeline in times of professional crisis. When my colleague attempted to derail my career, it was the strength of my reputation—built on these three pillars—that ultimately saved me.

As you move forward in your own branding journey, remember these lessons:
- Cultivate your Mental Wealth relentlessly. Your mindset is the seed from which all else grows.
- Nurture your Social Wealth intentionally. Every connection is an opportunity, every interaction a chance to reinforce your brand.

- Leverage your Financial Wealth strategically. Your expertise has value—learn to articulate and monetize it.

In the end, personal branding isn't just about survival in the professional world—it's about thriving. It's about creating opportunities rather than waiting for them. It's about building a reputation so strong that it precedes you, opening doors and creating a buffer against professional setbacks.

Imagine your personal brand as a tree. The roots are your authentic self, your values, and your unique experiences. These are nourished by your mental wealth – the confidence and self-assurance we discussed earlier. As you grow in self-awareness and shed your "liedentity," these roots deepen, providing a stable foundation for your brand.

The trunk of your tree is your core message and expertise. This is where your thought leadership comes into play. By consistently sharing valuable insights and perspectives, you strengthen this central pillar of your brand.

The branches represent the various platforms and networks where you express your brand. Your LinkedIn profile, your blog, your job, your speaking engagements – each of these extends your reach and influence. The leaves are your content – the articles, posts, and interactions that give life to your brand and attract your audience.

Finally, the fruit of your tree is the opportunities, connections, and impact you create. This is where your social wealth flourishes, as you build meaningful relationships and contribute value to your professional community.

Just as a tree needs consistent care to thrive, your personal brand requires ongoing attention and nurturing. The strategies we've discussed for creating captivating content are like the sunlight and water that help your brand grow. By avoiding the three major pitfalls we identified, you're protecting your brand from pests and disease that could stunt its growth.

A strong personal brand isn't built overnight. It's a process of continuous growth and adaptation. As you implement these strategies, you'll find that each element reinforces the others. Your increased confidence makes your content more compelling. Your thought leadership opens doors to new networking opportunities. Your authentic self-expression attracts like-minded professionals and opportunities that align with your values.

Now that you understand how these concepts interconnect, it's time to put them into action. Remember, knowledge without application is merely potential. Let's break down some concrete steps you can take to start building your personal brand today:

- **Audit Your Current Brand:** Take stock of your online presence. Google yourself. What comes up? Is it an accurate representation of who you are and what you offer? Make a list of areas that need improvement.
- **Create a Content Calendar:** Plan out your content for the next month. Aim for a mix of original posts, shared articles with your insights, and engagement with others' content.
- **Network Intentionally:** Reach out to one new person in your industry each week. Offer value before asking for anything in return.
- **Practice Confidence-Building Exercises:** Implement daily affirmations or visualization techniques to boost your mental wealth.
- **Seek Speaking Opportunities:** Look for chances to present at

- work, local meetups, or industry events. Start small and build up.
- **Engage in Continuous Learning:** Set aside time each week to stay updated on industry trends and develop new skills.

The strategies and insights we've explored are foundational, but the world of personal branding is ever-evolving, just like your own career and aspirations.

Consider this the first chapter in your ongoing story of professional development. As you implement these strategies and begin to see results, you'll naturally discover new areas for growth and exploration. Embrace this journey with curiosity and enthusiasm.

Here are some paths you might consider as you continue to develop your personal brand:

- **Deepen Your Expertise:** As you establish yourself as a thought leader, you may find specific areas where you want to develop deeper knowledge. Consider advanced certifications, specialized training, or even pursuing further education in your field.
- **Expand Your Reach:** Once you're comfortable with your personal brand on platforms like LinkedIn, explore other channels. This could include starting a podcast or be a guest on a podcast, creating video content, or writing for industry publications.
- **Build Your Own Platform:** As your following grows, you might consider creating your own community. This could be a membership site, a forum, or even a mastermind group where you facilitate connections and discussions among professionals in your field.
- **Mentor Others:** As you gain experience in personal branding,

- consider mentoring others who are just starting their journey. This not only helps others but also reinforces your own knowledge and positions you as an expert.
- **Write a Book:** Building on the thought leadership you've established, consider authoring a book on your area of expertise. This can be a powerful tool for further establishing your credibility and expanding your influence.
- **Develop Products or Services:** Your personal brand can be a springboard for creating products or services that serve your audience. This might include online courses, coaching programs, or digital tools related to your expertise.
- **Cross-Industry Collaboration:** Look for opportunities to apply your expertise in adjacent fields. This cross-pollination of ideas can lead to innovative insights and expand your network in exciting new directions.

The beauty of personal branding is that it evolves with you. As you grow and change, your brand will too.

As we walked through each chapter:
- **A**mplify Your Inner Confidence
- **N**avigate LinkedIn Confidently
- **S**culpt Your Unique Brand Identity
- **W**rite Your Success Story
- **E**mpower Your Skillset: Monetizing Your Expertise on LinkedIn
- **R**eel Them In: Mastering Attention-Grabbing LinkedIn Content

We've discovered that your personal branding journey isn't just about followers or likes. Your success in your career isn't about the value that someone places on you. Your wealth is no one else's responsibility but yours. It's about finding your voice, owning your expertise, and showing up as your authentic self in a world that desperately needs more genuine people. You are the **A.N.S.W.E.R.** – Always have been, always will be.

In the quiet moments before dawn, when the world still slumbers, there's a whisper that echoes through the corridors of possibility. It speaks of untapped potential, of dreams yet unfulfilled, of a voice yearning to be heard. That whisper, dear reader, is yours.

Your journey through these pages has been more than a mere traversal of words and strategies. It's been a pilgrimage to the core of your professional identity. You've unearthed the raw materials of your personal brand—now it's time to sculpt your masterpiece.

LinkedIn isn't just a platform; it's your canvas. Each post, each comment, each connection is a brushstroke in the portrait of your professional self. But remember, the most captivating artworks aren't those that shout for attention—they're the ones that resonate with truth, authenticity, and purpose.

There will be days when doubt clouds your vision, when the enormity of the digital landscape makes you feel insignificant. In those moments, recall this truth: every expert was once a beginner, every influencer once stood where you stand now. The difference? They chose to begin, to persist, to evolve.

You carry within you a unique alchemy of experiences, skills, and insights. This combination, this essence of you, is the solution to a problem that someone out there is grappling with right now. Your voice is the answer to a question that hasn't yet been articulated. Your presence on LinkedIn isn't just about building a brand—it's about creating connections that could alter the course of careers, companies, perhaps even industries.

As you close this book, know that this is not an ending, but a commencement. The real work, the true test, lies not in the reading, but in the doing. Your LinkedIn profile awaits your touch, your network hungers for your contributions, and yes—should you need guidance along the way, I stand ready to help you navigate these waters. The world doesn't just need what you have to offer—it deserves it. In an age of noise and distraction, your authentic voice has the power to cut through the chaos, to inspire, to lead, to transform. The question is no longer whether you have something valuable to share, but whether you have the courage to share it.

This moment is the intersection of all you've learned and all you're capable of becoming. The choice to step forward isn't just an opportunity; it's a responsibility to your future self and to every life you're meant to impact.

Your personal brand isn't just waiting to be built—it's an essential thread in the tapestry of our collective future. Will you weave it boldly? The digital stage is set, the professional world is watching, and history has a space reserved for trailblazers like you.

Now, take a deep breath. Feel the weight of this book in your hands one last time. Then set it down, pick up your device, and take that first, crucial step. Your remarkable journey awaits, and it begins now.

Promote Your D@mn Self!

Because if you don't the who will?!

Printed in Dunstable, United Kingdom